Sufism, Mahdism and Nationalism

Also available from Continuum

Christianity in Africa and the African Diaspora, edited by Roswith Gerloff, Klaus Hock and Afe Adogame

South Asian Sufis, edited by Charles M. Ramsey and Clinton Bennett

Sufism, Mahdism and Nationalism

Limamou Laye and the Layennes of Senegal

Douglas H. Thomas

continuum

Continuum International Publishing Group

The Tower Building
11 York Road
London
SE1 7NX

80 Maiden Lane
Suite 704
New York
NY 10038

www.continuumbooks.com

British Library Cataloguing-in-Publication Data
A catalogue record for this book is available from the British Library.

ISBN: HB: 978-1-4411-6907-5

Library of Congress Cataloging-in-Publication Data
Thomas, Douglas H., 1975—
Sufism, Mahdism and nationalism: Limamou Laye and the Layennes of Senegal/Douglas Thomas.
p. cm.
Includes bibliographical references and index.
ISBN 978-1-4411-6907-5 (hardcover)
1. Laye, Seydina Mouhamadou Lim?mou, 1845-1909.
2. Muslims–Senegal–Biography. 3. Sufism–Senegal–History.
4. Islam–Senegal–History. 5. Mahdism–History. I. Title.
BP80.L25T46 2011
297.4'8–dc23
[B] 2011031351

Typeset by Deanta Global Publishing Services, Chennai, India
Printed and bound in Great Britain

Contents

Acknowledgements

This work started ten years ago after having discussed the Layenne tariqa and its beliefs with my wife Fatou. I had just completed my master's thesis which was a comparative study of Sheikh Ahmadu Bamba Mbacke and Bishop Charles Harrison Mason. The discussion led to more investigations, which in turn led to a decision to study about Limamou Laye and his tariqa. I quickly discovered during my field work that the Layennes are a lot less comfortable discussing their tariqa and their beliefs than the Murides were. In spite of the frustration this caused, I continued on with the encouragement of my friends and family as well as scholars that I met along the way.

As an American Christian engaged in the study of Islamic practice and theology in Africa, this journey was as much one of self-discovery as it was of academic pursuit. I would like to first honour and thank the Almighty creator who never ceases to amaze me through his wondrous creations; my Lord Jesus Christ whose redemptive work on the cross is ever in my thoughts challenging my tendency to be intolerant as I'm ever reminded that while we were yet sinners, Christ died for us. I thank my parents and grandparents all of whom first sparked my interest in the divine through their patient teachings. I applaud my father for attempting to answer my question when at a young age I asked him about God's origin. I thank my maternal grandfather who took the time to teach me the twenty-third Psalm when I was just a small boy of four years; my paternal grandfather for insisting that I recite the Lord's prayer every night; and my mother and maternal grandmother for slowly and painstakingly teaching me their interpretation of God and the application of the said interpretation to their lives. I also thank the pastors Fred Pellum and Thomas Kennedy and their respective congregations.

I thank my high school world history teacher who spent two weeks on Islam and taken his time to give us information that was not in the textbook which sparked a passionate interest that continues to grow and expand over the years. Of all the Muslim friends I've met over the past twenty years, who broadened my understanding with their personal explanations of their faith and practice, none stands out like my friend Jaffar Muhammad Idrissa Toure. Many long conversations that often spilled over into the early hours of the morning during my undergraduate years gave a human face to the concept of Islam and Muslims because of his descriptions of his life 'back home' in Niger.

There are many academics who nurtured my interest and encouraged me. To name them all would take up more pages than my text. Some who stand out are Theman Taylor, Maurice Webb, Patricia McGraw, and Norbert Schoedler (who taught us to question everything) and Rick Scott, Stephen Webre, Jim Daly, Mamadou Diouf (who responded to my emails when as a graduate student I reached out to him and in one telephone conversation broadened my conceptualization of race and the progress of Islam in Africa putting questions on my mind many of which I'm still grappling to answer), Mohamed H. Ali (my patient dissertation advisor who quietly and patiently encouraged me), Cora Presley, and Carrie Manning. My colleagues and former colleagues at Atlanta Metropolitan College, Southern Arkansas University, and Grambling State University particularly the library staff many of whom were encouraging and/or patient, special thanks to Claudell Woods, Ben Johnson, Betty McCollum, and Roshunda Belton; Cheikh at the IFAN archives in Senegal, and every archive staff person who may have had to endure my impatience and frustration at the archives in Paris and Dakar. I also thank my good friend Amy Sy who often strayed from her medical studies to read parts of this work, SSD, Serigne Thierno Mbacke, Serigne Issachar Mbacke, Asta Souare, Anta Souare, As Dianka, Ahmadou Ka, Sulaiman Ndiaye, and countless others who discussed Islam in Senegal and enlightened me on finer points of the culture over many cups of ataaya. Last but definitely not least, I want to thank my ever-patient and encouraging wife Fatou (who herself is a fount of information and a good sounding board) and our four children Oliver, Binta, Jeremiah, and Rose whose calls to my office requesting that I pick up some treat reminded me when I'd been in the office too long. I thank all others who I could not name for lack of space and time, but who were instrumental in the completion of this work.

Introduction

On 24 May 1883, Libasse Chaw, recovering from the grief of his mother's death, proclaimed himself the reincarnation of the Prophet Muhammad. This proclamation was followed by miracles and another interpretation that Libasse Chaw, now called Limamou Laye (derivation of al-Imam Allah, or the imam of God), was *al-mahdi* or the rightly guided one predicted in Islamic eschatological teachings. When the larger picture is examined, the proclamation of a *Mahdi* is not unique to Libasse Chaw or his people, the Lebu. There were several men who proclaimed themselves *Mahdi* throughout the Muslim world. Limamou Laye's proclamation was based on a claim of reincarnation that is uncommon in Islamic theology. He also proclaimed himself the prophet of Islam, which is also against the basic tenets of the faith. Why would a lifelong Muslim articulate his message and couch it in terms of reincarnation? What in his environment led to the creation of such a *Mahdi*?

In this study, we argue that there are three historical forces that converged upon Senegambia and the surrounding regions. These three forces are Sufism, Mahdism, and nationalism. As historical forces, they are ideas that are accompanied by practices that lead men to change their worlds. This study covers circa 1850–1940. Conventional analyses treat this period in African History as one dominated by European conquest and subsequent colonization. This line of thinking is narrow, failing to take into account the precolonial history of Africa (and more pointedly Senegambia) and the forces at play in the unfolding of that history. Sufism's tenure in Senegambia predates European contact as do Mahdism and nationalism. These historical forces simply collided with European colonization. European colonization is not a historical force but an event that is the consequence of historical forces, that is, industrialization, capitalism, and its driving impetus, greed. The effects of Sufism, Mahdism, and nationalism are understudied and underappreciated. This study seeks to fill that gap.

Mahdism came along with Sufism in the flourishing of Islam. The Qur'an does not articulate specific eschatological details. The collections of Hadith, Sufi scholars, and popular belief combined to fill in the gaps. Mahdism evolved from this process. Al-Mahdi is the rightly guided one. The idea is that he is to come at the end of time to defeat evil along with Issa (Jesus Christ) and Muhammad. The Mujadid or reformer of Islam who comes at the turn of each Islamic century has a different role from that of the Mahdi. The Mahdi's arrival should signal the coming of the end. In practice, however, many claimants of the Mahdi title have exhibited characteristics of a Mujadid. Mahdism as a set of practices and belief is a messianistic ideology whereby those who participate look for a particularly gifted personage to come on to their scene and right all the wrongs. This ideology lends itself to an initial passiveness that bursts into action once the rightly guided one is identified and fully recognized by his powers. Being that the idea of the Mahdi sprung from popular belief, it has different versions throughout the Islamic world. The original Mahdist concept came from the Shia sects of Islam and was later appropriated by Sunni Muslims. The Shia Mahdi must be a descendent of Ali and will be the reappearance of the hidden caliph. The Sunni Mahdi can be any man who exhibits the qualities of a rightly guided scholar/leader, but he must have the name of the prophet. The Lebu interpreted Mahdi as a messianic figure who would meet their particular set of nationalistic needs.

The nationalism that we discuss here is ethnic nationalism that is not to be confused with the nationalism based upon the modern nation-state, though the latter evolved from the former in Europe. In Africa, the nationalism based on the modern nation-state did not have the chance to evolve nor is there any indication that it would have ever evolved. Modern African nation-states were artificially created by European colonizers. Very few of them have boundaries similar to the precolonial states that they replaced. When casual Western observers hurl the charge of tribalism at troubled African nations, I laugh at the irony of it all. Quite frankly, African countries are a lie coming from a grander falsehood of white supremacy, which was the guiding force of European colonization. As such, their nation-state nationalism is constructed from nothingness. Ethnic nationalism is still the prevailing identity. Unlike the hastily constructed codes and ethos of the modern African nation-state, ethnic nationalism was compiled over centuries and is supported with stories that are repeated to each generation. Unlike the falsehood of the modern African nation-state, ethnic nationalism is based on an ethos bound by the sacred. African ethnicities claim a common ancestor or experience whose origin sits at the beginning of time and is fully wrapped up in Divine will. As such, African ethnic nationalism is a religious idea and often reacted violently when confronted with the uniting impulse of Islam. Over time, this confrontation has evolved into an increasingly benign negotiation. The confrontation between ethnic nationalism and the nation-state, however, is anything but benign and nowhere near negotiation. Ethnic nationalism challenges the legitimacy of the nation-state. Like the layers of an onion, ethnic nationalism peels back the levels of the modern African nation-state only to find emptiness.

Islam came to sub-Saharan Africa in the 8th century. By the 10th century, Islam had firmly entrenched itself as a court religion and was gradually spreading throughout the rural areas. Nehemia Levtzion aptly describes the process when he wrote that "the Islamization of Africa became more successful because of the Africanization of Islam."[1] In other words, Islam as an "outside" force negotiated with the African social, cultural, and political norms in order to gain a place. Lamin Sanneh describes the initial stage as one of enclavement in which Islamic communities moved into non-Islamic areas with the blessings of the political leaders and established "enclaves" of Muslim activity.[2] This stage lasted for various periods depending on the place, but after the enclavement period progressive Islamization ensued often involving a renegotiation whereby more orthodox Islamic practices were interposed into the wider society while focal points of the religion were localized, hence the "Africanization of Islam." The question of agents of Islamization has gripped historiographical debate for the last decade. Scholars agree that the jihadist and other Islamic leaders were obvious agents of Islamization, but

Levtzion and others question the role of traders. Yet the role of the Joola traders and the schools and mosques that they established throughout the Western Sudan cannot be ignored. Sanneh points to the Jakhanke and the example that they established as peaceful rural agents of Islamization to counterpoint the overconcentration on jihadists in the literature. Agency is important, and thus cannot be oversimplified. I argue that native rulers, Muslim traders, and Islamic teachers as well as jihadists were agents of Islamization. The object of my study fit neither of these roles. On the contrary, he was an illiterate fisherman who had been raised a Muslim in a society where Islamization came late.

In addition to the larger argument that Mahdism, Sufism, and nationalism were the forces that created Limamou Laye, this study seeks to examine the renegotiation of Islam in the Lebu community of Senegal at the hands of Libasse Chaw, aka Limamou Laye. We argue that Limamou Laye's success was dependent on his ability to encapsulate his message in the tools of Lebu public discourse, which, in turn, lay in his position as first and foremost a Lebu and secondly a Muslim. Taking Limamou Laye's mission to the Lebu as a model, the study also analyzes what Islamization entails, that is, how it changes the native religious structures, the traditional social and political institutions, and thereby the role of women. The study also analyzes the Africanization of Islam in the Lebu context through which local cultural, political, and spiritual expression were accorded a place in Islam. Lebu nationalism was not cast aside, trampled, or simply covered with a veneer of Islam. Limamou Laye's tariqa bring Lebu nationalism into direct conversation with Islam. Islam responds in a language that resonates with Lebu culture, namely, Islamic mysticism expressed in Sufism and Mahdism.

The above-mentioned historical forces also unfolded within the context of a more intimate conflict between the global and the local. Sufism and Mahdism are evident throughout the Islamic world, and both had their beginning in local contexts as results of adapting global Islam to local realities. Nationalism is a human phenomenon which glorifies the local as a response to the localization of the global. The story of Limamou Laye is a case study of how Islam and the local realities negotiated their metaphysical and psychological space. This negotiation is ongoing with "orthodox" Islam increasingly gaining ground, but as long as the locals speak and think in their vernacular, Islam will always be filtered through the nationalist sieve. In this light, Limamou Laye's mission and message become paradoxical in that they request a paradigmatic shift but communicated through the language and modes of the existing paradigm. He argues that the Lebou can and should be good exclusive Muslims but he exploits the traditional belief system's codes and signs to propagate his message. Thus, the belief in reincarnation is presented in order to bring Muhammad and Issa into the Lebou family showing that God is a direct responder to the Lebou. Lebu nationalism responds directly to the Arab chauvinism of the Islamic world. Limamou Laye obviously sees Muhammad as a prophet to the world who came by way of the Arabs and who came again by way of the Lebu.

Little to no pre-Islamic religious ideas could survive Islamic legalism without the conduit of Sufism. Islamic mysticism, commonly called Sufism, emanates from a rather simple idea that a more profound experience with Allah is available. This idea suggests that there was something lacking in the pre-Sufi practice of Islam. In light of the history of Islam up to the 9th century, which is when Sufism appeared, orthodoxy and legalism dominated many other contradictory practices and beliefs. Beginning with Uthman's canonization of the Qur'an, Islamic political authorities sought to unite the Arab and non-Arab Muslims under one orthodox banner. With the development of *fiqh* in light of the Sunnah and the Qur'an, a legalistic aspect of Islam evolved and hardened. Sufism coming in the 9th century served as a spiritual counterbalance. There were those who sought to escape from the turmoil of Umayyad Caliphate through spiritual experience. Over time, experiential knowledge of Allah has been the guiding principle of Sufi leaders everywhere, and the rule of a seeker's submission to his spiritual master eventually replaced the original form of Sufism in which an individual sought Allah with little to no official guidance. Sufi *tariqas* (or paths) sprung up over time and spread throughout the Muslim world. Those that came to Senegambia were first the Qadiriya founded by Abd al-Qadir al-Jilani in Baghdad in the 10th century. Later, the Tijinayya was founded by Ahmed al-Tijani in Fez in the 18th century and spread almost immediately to sub-Saharan West Africa. Sufism has been the conduit for the spread of Islam throughout Western Africa and much of the world. Mystical beliefs and practices are major parts of traditional African religious systems. Mystical Islam was obviously appealing to this area. In Senegal, two Sufi groups were founded without any affiliation to another preexisting organization. These two are the Muridiyya and the Layennes. Both grew out of specific cultural and historical conditions.

Colonization has often been described as the defining factor in the spread of Islam in the Senegambia region. Less attention has been paid to the preexisting political conditions that led to the spread of Islam. The upheavals resulting from the slave trade directly connected to the introduction of guns and other weapons negatively affected the population putting the traditional authority structure in disarray. The preexisting understanding of the world was challenged and significantly adapted to the evolving situation. These are the conditions in which Islam spread. Sufism as a conduit was successful because of its easy collaboration with the esoteric focus of the traditional African world view.

The *tariqa* that resulted from Limamou Laye's proclamation has been largely ignored by scholars of Islam in West Africa. This neglect is mainly because the tariqa is so small and has been limited to Senegal, more pointedly, mostly to a small part of Senegal and largely to one ethnic group, the Lebu, though it spread to the Wolof. Only one study has been published on this tariqa by Cecile Laborde. It was her Master's thesis that developed into a book. Her focus was the idiosyncrasies of the tariqa and its relationship vis-à-vis the traditional religion and its practitioners. Our focus is the founder and the environment that created him.

Limamou Laye was a Lebu. The Lebu live on the Cap-Vert Peninsula. Prior to colonization, the Kingdom of Cayor claimed the Lebu area as a province. The Lebu, however, always lived in relative isolation, thus the pattern of Islamization was slower for the Lebu than for the other parts of Senegambia. Islamic traders from the Maghreb had come among the Lebu early in their history (ca 14th century), yet there are no report of communities of rural Islamic teachers establishing communities among the Lebu as in other parts of

Senegambia. Thus Islam, though present, was not a strong vital force until the arrival of Jaal Joop.

Fleeing the wrath of Amary Ngoone Ndeela, the *Dameel* (king) of Cayor, after an unsuccessful jihad in 1795, Jaal Joop and his followers fled to Lebu where he quickly established himself as an Islamic leader and married into the native population. Native Lebu religious leaders were mostly women who were also in control of religious education in that society. Joop and others married native women. With such hands rocking their cradles, a strict adherence to Islam was compromised in the Joop family and others. Jaal Joop's role in regularization of Islam in the Lebu community cannot be overlooked, however unsuccessful it may seem. One of the themes of my argument is that there are many Islams. The renegotiation of Islam has as its goal to move the local Islam as close to the ideal orthodox Islam as possible. Thus, a different Islam results from each negotiation. As more members of the community become attracted to the Islamic religious ideal, a renegotiation is necessary.

Mitigating circumstances such as the role of women and traditional religion mentioned above often served as important factors in the mode and means of Islamization. Sanneh calls for a new mode of analysis based on the responsiveness of Islam to Africa's religious traditions.[3] My focus on negotiation evolved from an analysis of responsiveness. In studying the spread of Islam in the Western Sudan, it is clear that Islamization is in constant discussion with the indigenous religious tradition as well as the traditional political and social institutions. Various aspects of both sides are downplayed or discarded at various moments as the relationship between both develops, thus a negotiation takes place. As situations change, i.e. Islam acquires more adherents or economic power, Islam's place is renegotiated vis-à-vis the indigenous society.

Most scholars of Islam in West Africa have not properly analyzed the precolonial governments' relationship with Islam and its link to how Islam spread during and after colonization. The prevailing assumption has been that the prevalence in eschatological Islamic proclamations throughout the world was connected to the change in the sociopolitical order connected to colonization. A distinct feature of many of the beliefs on the *Mahdi* and the *Mujahedeen* was the belief in the appearance of a renewer at the end of each century. The end of the 19th century on the Gregorian calendar was the beginning of the 14th century Hegira. Muslims who were looking for hope in their religion were looking for the fulfillment of the prophecy. Yet, scholars blinded by the "light" of colonization tread the path that Laborde did when she declared that the colonization was the stimulus for the progress of Islamization. Beginning with the jihad of the Almoravides in the 11th century, violently aggressive Islamization has disrupted the social order of Senegambia. After much of the area was Islamized, the disruptions did not cease as El Hajj Omar Tall and others emerged claiming that the Muslims were not Muslim enough. Added to the religious spin on the conflicts was the New World's growing demand for African slaves that led enterprising individuals to steal and sometimes wage war in order to increase their bottom line. These disruptions were sufficient to make the believers look for the Mahdi.

Most works on Islam in West Africa, particularly Senegambia, have concentrated mainly on specific leaders and their relationships with colonizers such as David Robinson's work on El-Hajj Umar Tall and Donal Cruse O'Brien's work on Sheikh Ahmadou Bamba Mbacké. Robinson's work is rich with information and contextualization. Though well researched, O'Brien's work and other works (like Trimingham's impressive volumes on Islam in Africa) rest on outdated assumptions posited in earlier works by Paul Marty, a French colonial official and chronicler of Islam in French West Africa among others. Chief among those assumptions is the idea that the Islam of sub-Saharan Africa was inferior to that of the Moors of North Africa. This racist postering obscures the record of violent disruption and its consequences.[4]

Other works on the general history of the region or parts of the region do give place for analysis of Islamization, such as Mamadou Diouf's monograph on Cayor, Boubacar Barry's works on Waalo and his survey of Senegambian history, and to a lesser degree Eunice Charles's work on Jolof. In these works, however, Islamization is a minor part of the works' focus.[5] The works which concentrate on Islamization, such as Levtzion's work cited above, seem to only recount the broader waves of Islamization while minimizing the nuances of the process. The role of the Jakhanke and their process which many other groups followed, is rarely if ever mentioned while most discussions concentrate on Islamic traders, Muslims in the royal courts, age of jihad, and the formation of turuq (religious orders, plural of tariqa) in the 19th century.[6] Hiskette's work and Peter Clarke's work, both on the Islamization of West Africa, while great resources on the broader movements also have limited space for a nuanced discussion.

Donal Cruise O'Brien and Christian Coulon's edited volume on charisma and African Islam is an example of this type of book. While their stated focus is the leadership of the turuq, the direction of the work is generally faulty in that it fails to accurately bring a coherent discussion of Weberian charisma in the various cases discussed. Their model of "not quite charisma" fails to address the question of the longevity of these organizations in the face of rapidly changing societies. David Robinson's work on accommodation describes the relationship between the French and the Islamic leaders/polity during colonization. David Searing's work gives a more nuanced discussion of the progress of Islam at the juncture of colonization, properly contextualizing colonization as just another event in the history of the region. Searing's work also tackles the issue of slavery and how the progress of Islam led to a dismantling of the institution. Though Searing's analysis is a positive advancement in the field, there are too few studies which caste aside the assumptions of the colonial governments and present a reassessment. My work seeks to fill the void in the literature. I will take the Lebu society as a microcosm of the wider Senegambian region and analyze how Islam progressed there. The role of Limamou Laye and the Layenne tariqa is central to the discussion in that it produced the renegotiation that made Islam central to the Lebu society, culture, and politics. The convergence of Sufism, Mahdism, and nationalism is the force that produces the renegotiation in Limamou Laye's work. As such, these three historical forces are central to our analysis.

Our study begins with a presentation of Islam, Muhammad, and Jesus. This chapter lays the basis for a greater analysis of Layenne beliefs and practices. The next chapter is a reexamination of the history of Islam in Western Africa from penetration to the advent of colonization that is used to historically contextualize the Limamou Laye and his tariqa. In chapter 3, we present a brief ethnology of the Lebu pointing out features that have contributed to the Layenne theology while tracing the history of the evolution of Lebu nationalism. Chapter 4 traces the early life of Libasse Chaw/Limamou Laye ending with the announcement. Chapter 5 continues with the life of Limamou Laye and the founding of the tariqa while critically analyzing how it was shaped and how it shaped the Lebu society, politics, and culture. Chapter 6 explains the continuation of the tariqa under the leadership of Seydina Issa Rohou Laye, Limamou Laye's son. Chapter 7 examines the state of Islam in present-day Senegal and the place of the Layenne tariqa in it. In these seven chapters, I hope to correct the unmentioned nuances of the development of Islam in West Africa as it faced other historical forces that transformed but not deformed it.

Chapter 1

Islam, Muhammad, Jesus and the World

While living in Liberia, I was walking one Saturday night on the campus of the rural university where I worked. A man approached me and asked me for a dollar to buy more beer. He reeked of palm wine and was visibly inebriated, so I reproached him for his behavior. In an attempt to play on his sense of religious responsibility, I added, "and you dishonor God by asking me in front of this chapel and getting drunk tonight. Will you be ready for church in the morning?" Clearly exasperated, he replied, "Why do you have to bring God into this?"

This seemingly simple question carries so much ideological and cultural baggage. Precolonial African religions exerted authority and concern for all areas of life. Colonization brought Western Christianity, which, in turn, brought the idea of the secular, that is, areas of existence outside the domain of religious thought and/or action. These gray areas were quickly filled with African traditional beliefs and practices that missionaries were quick to renounce but nearly impossible to eradicate even after over a century of colonial and neocolonial cultural genocide. Though on life support, traditional African religions are not dead.

Benjamin Ray defines religion as "a complex of ideas and practices that gives ultimate meaning to human existence and enhances the quality of life." If we are to subscribe to that definition, what is the purpose of the secular? The secular is a relatively new concept whose origin lies in the so-called European Enlightenment. Religion is indeed a complex of ideas and practices that encompasses the life of the believer and gives meaning to that life. This concept of religion supersedes mere rules and regulations and extends to one's way of thinking and behaving. In order for Westerners to analyze Islam or

African religious life, we must first rid ourselves of the notion of the secular and begin afresh. With this in mind, we turn to Islam.

Islam came to Africa centuries before Western Christianity. Unlike Western Christianity, Islam has rules to govern every area of life and seeks to fundamentally alter one's worldview by realigning the cosmos in a way that Western Christianity failed to do. Islam did not seek to replace the traditional African gods. Islam sought to destroy those gods and everything associated with them. Much like the initial onslaught of Christianity in Western Europe, many African beliefs and practices have been transformed to accommodate Islam as have many Islamic practices crossed into traditional African religions. Over the centuries, however, with rounds of Islamic renewal campaigns (both violent and peaceful), the practice of Islam has come closer to the orthodox ideal. Yet there remains a worldview that is as intensely African as it is Islamic. For some, the belief in the supremacy of Muhammad's prophetic office does not stand at odds to the belief in righting wrongs through maraboutic magic. For many, praying five times a day does not seem to conflict with the practice of leaving milk out for family spirits. The personal attraction of Islam's message runs counter to the cultural specificity of its medium, which continues to leave large areas of spiritual practice uncovered.

Islam as a belief evolved over centuries into an international religion that has successfully obliterated traditional geographical and cultural barriers. The rapid successful spread of Islam cannot be overlooked or easily explained away in an age when communication and travel were long, arduous, and perilous. The system of broadcasting the message along with the formulation of the message has been instrumental in the success of Islam. In this chapter, we will analyze the history, formation, and formulation of Islam as a historical and theological force.

Islam: The Beginning

Conventional wisdom tells us that Islam began when Muhammad received his first revelation. The Qur'an, however, describes Islam as a continuation of Judaism and an answer to Christianity with the understanding that the Jews and Christians had contorted the message, thereby making them unworthy.[1] So Islam is proclaimed as the one true religion which by definition predates Muhammad's revelation. This perception of Islamic theological history sets the timbre of the evolution of the religion. Islam ceases to be something new and just a repackaging of a primordial communication from the creator to a new people and a reminder to all others. The arching question arises about Muhammad's position. Can he be just another messenger for the same message from God? The essence of the message is clear: submit to the will of God. It is essentially the same message that Moses pushed and the other Jewish prophets came to reinforce that message. Moses stands out as the lawgiver and thereby the solidifier of the covenant first between Abraham and God and then between Jacob's children and God. Though Moses is a lawgiver, the tragic cadences of Jeremiah's warnings, the steadfastness of Daniel, and the regretful story of Jonah among others still stand out to give an often cruel poetic substance to the essential message.

In Islam, there would be no Daniel or a lion's den, no Jonah's whale, and no mournful lamentations from an Islamic Jeremiah. Muhammad ended the revelations with his person. Once Islam went global, not only was Muhammad the last Arab prophet, but also the last prophet of the world. This change catapulted Muhammad from a mere conduit of the message to the Arabs to the unique prophet of the world. This change also repositioned Muhammad to the center of Islam. As messenger, he is essential to Islam. It is no wonder that early-on Europeans called Muslims Muhammadans, or followers of Muhammad. Before we delve into Muhammad's positioning in the Islamic cosmos, we must first revisit the founding of the religion.

In 610, Muhammad retreated to the caves above Mecca for meditation. While there he said he received his first revelation from the angel Jibreel. From this initial revelation, he received people who believed in his proclamations. This put him at variance with the citizens of Mecca who had become rich from the worship of gods and goddesses at the Kaba in Mecca. He was protected by his grandfather Abdul-Mutalib who also raised Muhammad. Once Abdul-Mutalib died, Muhammad's uncle, Abu Talib, became his protector. Eventually, Muhammad's proclamations against polytheism led to him and his followers being persecuted and emigrating to Yathrib, later known as *al-Madīnah l-Munawwarah* or the radiant city, today known as simply Medina. The people of Yathrib asked Muhammad to come and settle a dispute that led to his change of headquarters. The people of Mecca pursued him, however, and even after the battle of Badr, where the people of Mecca were defeated, their harassment continued. City by city, the Muslims conquered the whole of the Arabian Peninsula culminating in the taking of Mecca where they cleaned out the Kaba and dedicated it solely to the worship of Allah. Shortly thereafter, Muhammad died.[2]

After all the challenges faced during Muhammad's lifetime, the test of the group's survival occurred during the first century after Muhammad's death. The first challenge was over the next leader. Muhammad's cousin, father-in-law, closest aide, Abu Bakr took the helm though many thought it should have gone to Ali, the cousin and son-in-law of Muhammad. Then there was the issue of orthodoxy and theological unity. There were bits and pieces of the revelations floating around the Ummah in addition to various versions. Uthman insisted that one version be used leading to the standardization of the text.[3]

Evolving Prophethood

Throughout the leadership of the first four caliphs and on into the Umayyad period, the warriors of Islam spread their rule throughout North Africa, the Middle East, Eastern Europe, and Western Europe as well as Central, and Eastern Asia. The spread of the faith from the Semetic context of two older more influential religions to new regions necessitated a reorientation of the faith. Muhammad obviously rose in esteem. One of the earliest biographies of Muhammad attempts to cast Muhammad in relation to other prophets that came before him. Written in the 760's by Ibn Ishaq, the *Sirat Rassul Allah* comprises three different parts. In the initial part *Kitab al-Mubtada*, Ibn Ishaq uses the stories of Biblical prophets as well as Arab prophets from the oral tradition. His use of the *Isra'iliyat*, collection of extra-Islamic accounts derived from Jewish sources, as well as the oral tradition contextualizes Muhammad in the world system. These sources are not strictly from the canonical texts, but they have an obvious origin in the Jewish sources. All the prophets in ibn Ishaq's work have the same message as Muhammad and the telling is structured in such a way as to crescendo towards the coming of Muhammad.[4] The end result is a new understanding of Muhammad and his mission. He ceased to be an Arab messenger with a mission to his people. He became a messenger for the world with an all-encompassing message. The Arab language and customs inherent in the practice of Islam did not disappear, however. The reorientation was more the result of new interpretations from new people with un-Arab cultures. The concretization of the message in the terms of the scholars did not always jibe with the emotional needs of the various adherents from different religious and spirituals backgrounds. A religion that could be felt was developed through mysticism of the early Sufis.

Sufism begins in Basra in the 8th century as a response to the perceived moral laxity of Islam. There were two stages of the development of Sufism. Similar to the monastic life in early Christianity, early Sufism had little to no structure and was practiced more or less on an individual basis. Within roughly a generation, Sufism underwent a process of institutionalization where the initial stage of asceticism gave way to a structured focus on reaching God spiritually. Imitating Muhammad was the acknowledged way of reaching God. It was at this point that Islamic prophethood morphed into a messianism. Muhammad was always seen as unique as a human being and a prophet. It was in Sufi belief and practice, however, where his life and actions were seriously studied and imitated.

It was in the 8th century that the use of "extra-Islamic" sources fell out of favor. Islamic sources for works on the religion were looked at as exclusive bearers of the truth.[5] Muhammad took the center stage of religious beliefs and practices along with the Qur'an. Eventually, the idea evolved that Muhammad was the first created being and only perfect being. Around 900, Tustari wrote that Muhammad was the first of God's three lights created. Ibn Arabi also wrote "love of the prophet leads to love of God." The popular belief evolved that even pronouncing Muhammad's name gave baraka. In comparison to all other previous prophets, Muhammad is on top. Echoing orthodox christology, Muhammad's existence was said to predate his descent among men. The argument emanated from the fact that Muhammad was the conduit of Islam. As such he was the perfect Muslim and as such he evolved in the minds into the perfect human being. So his personality was not a conduit to God, but the only conduit to God.[6]

Schimmel argues that the beliefs and practices of what she calls Muhammad mysticism run counter to Muhammad's wish that a personality cult does not develop around him. She also argues that Muhammad is not a part of Islam's foundational phenomenon. Whatever the case, Muhammad mysticism spread throughout the Islamic world. By the late 11th and early 12th centuries, the celebration of Muhammad's birthday spread along with the popular belief that Muhammad will be the intercessor on doomsday emanating from a Qur'anic verse that reads "We have sent you out of mercy from us towards the whole world." The prevailing interpretation was that Muhammad was that mercy.[7]

These developments coincided with Islam's spread into the areas that were formally Christian. Christological elements were included into Muhammad mysticism that culminated in the changing of Muhammad from prophet to messianic figure. This was not a turning of theological focus from Allah and the Qur'an. On the contrary, Muhammad's importance was evidenced in his connection between Allah and the revealed word. This new theological arrangement, however, spread all over the world with Sufism. As Islam spread into areas that were previously Christian, there was an inevitable comparison between Jesus and Muhammad. With the pressures resulting from the wars between Muslims and Christians, another parallel public relations war of sorts raged between practitioners on both sides of the divide starting with a basic comparison of Jesus and Muhammad. The mysticism that developed around Muhammad quickly answered the comparisons.

Jesus and Islamic Eschatology

The role of Jesus in Islam is not as clearly defined as that of Muhammad. Jesus is understood to be a prophet, the offspring of Mariama, but definitely not the son of God. The Qur'an is clear in declaring that Allah has no children or a wife. It goes on to say that those who proclaim that Allah has a son do not know Him.[8] The Qur'an also says Jesus was not crucified but taken up to God.[9] With those two stipulations, the strength of Christianity is stricken. Without Jesus being the son of God, he is demoted to a prophet. A monophysite Christian could accept this condition, but once the crucifixion is taken away, Christianity is gone. The idea of all sins being answered at the cross is the binding belief of the Christian faith. However, after setting out the major difference between the two religions, Islamic doctrine accords Jesus respect as a prophet even giving him a place in the eschatology developed after the death of Muhammad.

The Qur'an does not offer a comprehensive eschatological narrative. There are descriptions of paradise complete with celestial virgins that "neither man nor jinn have touched." There is also mentioning of the horrors of hell.[10] However, a comprehensive description of the end of times is not in the Qur'an. Islam's view of the end of times is not as neatly and cogently described as what we find in the book of Revelations. The compilation of Hadith and other extra-Qur'anic literature attempt to fill the void. Yet, the story of the end times is scattered throughout the Qur'an, collections of Hadith, and other scholarly writings. Some scholars have scanned the sources and pieced together eschatological narratives. The end result is that most Muslims have a general idea of what will happen at the end of the world, but the details of the story vary depending on who is relating the narrative.

Islam needed an eschatological account because as the major competitor in the religious sphere, Christianity had one already articulated in their canonical scripture. The evolution of the eschatology was also necessary to bring closure to the Islamic spiritual journey. It had to be created because as Islam spread, it reached people all over the world who needed to make sense of the world as a whole. Just as the character of Muhammad had to change from one of an Arab prophet to his people, so did the message require additions to make sense to those who understood Christianity and saw themselves as citizens of a world beyond their immediate geography.

The oral tradition developed an eschatology that involves Jesus, Dajjal (the deceiver or anti-Christ), and the Mahdi in addition to Muhammad. In one version, the Mahdi returns to earth to reinstitute the golden age of Islam. Dajjal will begin his onslaught against the believers. Just as they prepare for war, Jesus will descend and be led in prayer by the Mahdi. Then Jesus will successfully defeat Dajjal in a war that occurs in Damascus. From that time on, Jesus will be king for 40 years during which Gog and Magog will invade the area only to meet defeat at the hand of Jesus with the help of Allah. At the end of his reign, Jesus will marry and have children and will be settled into domestic life for 19 years before dying and being buried next to Muhammad. Thus, the opposing characters in the religious/ideological wars will be joined in death.

It is clear that the writers of the story borrowed from Christian sources when relating the details of the end times. This is not to say that these scholars went out of their way to find Christian sources. The reality is that there were many Christian and Jewish ideas that had been traveling around the Middle East for centuries and had thereby entered the realm of commonly held belief. Islamic scholars most likely grew up hearing the details of the Christian eschatology narrative being told in various editions on any given occasion. The manner in which such eschatological material is presented in various collections of Hadith suggests that they have not come from a serious study of any particular writing. They are more or less alluded to as if the audience is expected to have a familiarity with them.

For example, in Sahih Bukari, Gog and Magog are presented in one saying attributed to Muhammad. "The Prophet said 'The people will continue performing the Hajj and 'Umra to the Ka'ba even after the appearance of Gog and Magog.'"[11] Gog and Magog are mentioned in the Bible. In Genesis, Gog and Magog appear on a list of nations descended from Noah's son Japheth after the flood. In Ezekiel and Revelations, they are mentioned as a huge armed force, multinational in Ezekiel, deceived by Satan in Revelations, which will come and battle God's people. Stories of this battle were probably discussed throughout the world with embellishments and extemporaneously added details. As part of the body of known things, the battle is referred to without explanation. The neat split between Islam, Christianity, and Judaism that we have concocted today was not the reality of an ancient world where ideas were in constant motion often traveling faster than the caravans that carried them. The speed of ideas is a major factor in what shaped Islamic eschatology and carried it into the farthest west corner of Africa.

Mahdism

Islamic eschatology is accompanied by signs. Scholars have identified minor signs and major signs. The eschatological narrative's details are so easily edited and left open to interpretation, the signs can be taken from any given situation in any given time. An ambitious leader could easily manipulate the fear of people, proclaim himself Mahdi, and carve out a position of power and wreak havoc in any land. This is what happened throughout the world. The driving force behind such events is an abiding belief by millions that the Mahdi is coming. We define this belief and the actions that prepare for the coming of an anointed one as Mahdism.

Messianic in nature and focus, Mahdism as a system of thought and action has as its ethos disgust with the present situation and a desire to change. It is no wonder that the poor and oppressed flock to Mahdist concerns. Any movement that has dissatisfaction at its heart will attract the dissatisfied along with their frustrations and contempt. In other words, Mahdism usually is coupled with violence. Not all Mahdist movements act in violence, but they are all by default of a violent rhetoric because their search for change is one of immediate change. Much like any revolutionary movement, Mahdism's stipulation of immediacy and urgency disrupts norms at all levels of society. Unlike secular revolutionary movements, however, Mahdism has divine endorsement that attracts even the satisfied, transforming them into the dissatisfied through an analysis of the status quo as a cause for God's displeasure.

In a purely materialistic society, Mahdism's appeal is not as strong with the rich believers as with the poor. In a situation where Mahdism finds even the rich believer without political power, its appeal is more potent. Invasions, conquest, colonization, and coup d'etats all create situations where riches do not translate into political power. The loss of cultural power can also drive many to Mahdism. For example, the influx of Western ideas into traditionally Islamic areas has led to the loss of influence of religious leaders who in turn invoke many traditionally Islamic beliefs to refocus the population on the leadership. Mahdism is just one weapon in an arsenal that includes conservative Islamism and terrorism.

The effectiveness of Mahdism is dependent not only on purely socioeconomic factors. Educational level is also a determinant of the potency of Mahdism. Access to an array of ideas, global travel, and interaction with people from other faiths and cultures will either drive an adherent into reactionary defense of his/her basic beliefs or lead to a reevaluation of them. One's tolerance is the deciding agent in this process. Mahdism can find adherents in a highly educated and globally conscious environment, but many of the basic tenets must be tweaked in order to be more palatable to such a populace.

Mahdism as a force of history, like any other messianic movement, can be a defining guide but only when the appropriate conditions exist. In 19th century Sudan, Muhammad Ahmad ibn Abd-Allah had a situation with all the appropriate conditions. He was in an area that had been ruled by outsiders sponsored by a discredited Islamic power, namely, Egypt. Furthermore, Egypt had allowed infidels to come in and directly control Sudan. Islamic leaders armed with scholarly arguments and righteous indignation lived in a separate sphere from a largely impoverished though pious populace. Because of Sufism, the leaders had the ability to mobilize the populace, but there were divisions between Sufi leaders and non-Sufi leaders as well as among Sufi leaders. Poverty and social marginalization combined in Muhammad al-Mahdi's favor and he urged the populace on to victory. He managed to hold them together until his death after which his top lieutenant held power until the divisive tribal politics began to tear at the fabric of his revolution along with his fool-hardy invasion of Ethiopia which though initially successful stretched his resources and capabilities beyond their limit.

The inevitable weakness with Muhammad Ahmad's position and that of his successor Abdulahi ibn Muhammad is the otherworldly baggage that comes with the Mahdi narrative, which will kill the revolution if it does not materialize quickly and in the eyes of everyone. There were not enough tangible miracles that could make the various tribes forget their old alliances and enemies. An impoverished and oppressed populace expects immediate relief from a divine revolution. When the relief fails to materialize, belief in the revolution fails. Hatred of the Egyptian suzerainty was the uniting force. Islam was just a thinly constructed net that served as an initial rallying point. Once the hated overlord was overthrown and Khartoum taken, the net of Islam proved insufficient to hold the coalition together.

Though ultimately unsuccessful, the Sudanese Mahdist state was a defining moment for the Sudanese and has served as an inspiration for many colonized people, Muslims and non-Muslims alike. As an example of Mahdism, the Sudanese Mahdist State speaks volumes about the power of Mahdism as a historical force while not ignoring that Mahdism saddled a nascent nationalism which in turn was undermined by tribalism. The larger lesson from this episode is not Mahdism's failure but the failure of Islam to unite people above and beyond their familial/tribal connections. Mahdism is an Islamic messianic movement and as such can only be as successful as Islam is. One could easily argue that Islam is split into believers and those who only pay lip service to the religion and it was this division that comprises the real problem. I however point to another weakness of Islam as a multi-tribal/mutli-cultural uniting force: Arab chauvinism.

Arab Chauvinism

Although Islam adjusted to a new status as a world religion in its first century, it never lost its organic Arab characteristics. The most telling of these characteristics is the retention of classical Arabic as the liturgical language. Arabic names are preferred. The Arabic language became sacred to non-Arab Muslims as it was also a conduit of God's revealed word for all humankind. Arabic is also a must for the initial and concluding parts of the prayer. Non-Arab Muslim children go through many pains (both literally and figuratively) to learn classical Arab in order to read and understand the Qur'an its original language.

In addition to the language, Mecca and Medina are pilgrimage points where Muslims must pass if they are able. This stipulation is a major anchor for this global religion to its local past. Along with the language stipulation and the ethnic origin of the founder, the idea that the real religion is found in the original place among the original people has subordinated the practice of non-Arabs and their practice and faith. This underlying assumption is shared among non-Muslims as well as in the Muslim world. A stronger issue with Arab chauvinism in Islam is the underlying psychological questions that it poses to the non-Arab adherent.

In Islam all prophets are either Jewish or Arab. Their warnings and words are delivered in their own languages to their own people. What does this say to the non-Arab people, particularly those who have proud heritages? In order to fuse the greatness of the tribe/family with that of Islam, many have resorted to *sherifism*, or the creation of genealogies that connect one's family to Muhammad's family. "The hadith states, The Prophet (peace_be_upon_him) said: The Mahdi will be of my family, of the descendants of Fatimah." Muhammad Ahmad used this technique to justify his claims as Mahdi. In Black Africa, there was an early attempt to connect to the prophet's first Black African follower, Bilal. This management of the psychological dissonance that Arab chauvinism creates does not deny the greatness of the Arab in the sacred practice of Islam, nor does it deny the greatness of the adherent's ancestry and ethnicity. However, that process still looks to the Arab as the greatest of all by saying that the adherent's family evolved from an Arab.

Another possible answer to this problem is to broaden one's view of the world and include himself/herself as a global citizen making the identification with Islam the most important connection in one's life. Even in this, the question arises, "If we are all equal before God, why did He choose an Arab to deliver his message to Arab people using an Arab language?" The persistent questions create a seemingly unsolvable problem. The assertion that Muhammad existed before his descent to earth in the body of an Arab coupled with the translation of the Qur'an into various languages helps to settle some of this issue; however, the insistence on the use of the Arab language and the perfection of an Arab as an example to the rest of humanity still persist in saying that all non-Arabs are just not good enough. Limamou Laye's movement answered Arab chauvinism.

Chapter 2

Islam in Senegal

This chapter gives an abbreviated history of Islam in West Africa in general and Senegambia specifically. We use Boubacar Barry's definition of Senegambia being present-day Southern Mauritania, Southwestern Mali, Senegal, Gambia, and Guinea-Conakry. We will trace the progress of Islamization from penetration to the 19th century.

Islamic Penetration and Expansion

Islam came to the Empire of Ghana in the 9th century. The initial penetration was peaceful, having come through trade. The emperor of Ghana allowed the Muslims to live in a quarter of the capital, Koumbi-Saleh. The Muslim traders served as secretaries and transcribers as well as religious leaders. Once the Empire of Mali began to fill the power vacuum left in the wake of Ghana's fall, Islam had become a mainstay of Western Africa's (which up until the 1960's was generally referred to as the Western Sudan) religious and social landscape.

Our goal in this work is to analyze the processes that made the "Islamization of Africa and the Africanization of Islam" in the Western Sudan generally and in Senegambia specifically, thereby providing a viable explanation for the evolution of the Islamic society that gave birth to the Mahdist Layenne tariqa. Thus, it is important that we look at two extremes of the diffusion process—violent conversion and peaceful conversion. We have no intention of pressing the false binary of either violent or peaceful, because there are all the variables between these two poles. However, for the sake of brevity and concision, we will limit our discussion to these two extremes. The pattern of Islamic expansion in the region was one of peaceful initial penetration, but purists and ambitious men who used the purists' argument organized violent reform movements in order to ensure conformity to the prominent idea of Islam. Along with the periodic violent jihads was the peaceful expansion of a stricter adherence to Islamic principles as independent ascetic institutions established Qur'an schools throughout the region. These processes are discussed in the following narrative.

Ghana and the Traders

In the 9th century, Islam was present in the ancient Empire of Ghana whose capital, Koumbi-Saleh, was just south of the Senegal River. Koumbi-Saleh was divided into two parts, one for the traditionalists and the other for Muslims. Initially, the Muslim community of Koumbi-Saleh consisted mainly of traders and a few native converts, but the settlers' income from trade brought them much influence as did their ability to write. The kings of Ancient Ghana practiced traditional religion, but they were reportedly accommodating to the Muslim traders, eventually converting to Islam. According to the sources, in the later part of the 11th century, the ruler converted to Islam. Because of their influence, the Muslim community grew in two ways. More Muslim traders came and established households taking wives from the native population and raising their children as Muslims. Natives also converted to Islam for a variety of reasons. This was the pattern of conversion that would be repeated in every kingdom in Western Africa. Muslims came in from another place, garnered influence, married into the indigenous population, and spread their faith to the natives. The end result was a population who interposed an essentially pre-Islamic cosmological understanding onto Islamic practice. Thus, the traditional African worldview remained the superstructure into which Islamic practice and theology was adapted.

Trade was an obvious conduit for Islam. The people of the Western Africa had been in contact with the Berbers of North Africa for centuries before Islam. When the Arabs brought Islam they tapped into the existing trade routes and expanded them. According to one story, the governor of Iffriqiya in present-day Tunisia organized a raiding expedition into the sub-Saharan area that netted such a large quantity of slaves and gold, that the governor had wells dug strategically along a path into Western Africa in order to facilitate trade.[1] With the gold coming in large quantities as well as salt and slaves, the Muslim traders created a network that crisscrossed Western Africa, connecting the region with Northwestern Africa and the rest of the world. In order to be a part of this network, one had to become a Muslim. Native merchants who wanted to expand into the new order converted.

Because of the lucrative trade, Arab and Berber traders began to settle in sub-Saharan capitals. As already mentioned, an Islamic quarter developed in Koumbi-Saleh and also in Gao and Takhrur. The result was expansion of Islam in the urban areas as well as along the trade routes starting with business partners and clients and eventually flowing into the royal courts. The Muslim traders showed themselves valuable as clerks as well as businessmen. With the establishment of Islamic communities came the development of Islamic scholarly communities. These scholars were usually behind a push for a more orthodox practice of Islam. Many of the early Berber converts to Islam followed the Ibadite branch of the Kharijite heresy[2], a grouping of Muslims who reject certain aspects of orthodox Islam. As the scholarly community expanded in Western Africa, it waged ideological and sometimes literal war against the Kharijite groups and others. The end result was a slate of conversions of native rulers. Around 1030, the Mandingo kingdom of Takhrur, just north of the Senegal River, was solidly Islamic and it influenced the Wolof lands to the South. Around 1200, Njaanjaan Njaay established the Kingdom of Jolof. Njaanjaan Njaay reportedly converted to Islam, which caused some uneasiness among the assembly of chiefs over which he ruled, though they eventually accepted his conversion.[3] Ghana's royal acceptance of Islam had something to do with the Almoravides.

The Almoravides

The Almoravides were a Muslim group from the Sanhaja Berbers who originated in present-day Mauritania. Abdullah Ibn Yasin al

Jazuli started this group in the first half of the 11th century. Yahya Ibn Ibrahim, chief of the Judullah branch of the Sanhaja, brought Ibn Yasin with him to teach a more orthodox Islam among the Judullah. Ibn Yasin's strict rules and obstinate attitude did not endear him to the Judullah. Jawhar Ibn Sakkum was a master of *fiqh* (Islamic Law) among the Judullah, and he took issue with Ibn Yasin's interpretation and administration of the law. Once the chief Yahya Ibn Ibrahim died, the rupture between Ibn Sakkum and Ibn Yasin spread to the followers, and ibn Yasin was ousted from power and forced to leave. Ibn Yasin went to the Lamtuna Berbers (another Sanhaja branch) and established a power base there. Later sources say he established a monastery like community on an island in the Senegal River, hence the name *murabitin* or people of the *ribat*, ascetic institution. There seems to be, however, no mention of this in the contemporary sources. All sources agree that the establishment of the movement was significant in that it grew into a formidable military force waging jihad on all their neighbors who practiced deviations in Orthodox Islam as well as the non-Islamic neighbors.[4]

Abdullah Yasin al-Ghazuli died fighting against the people of Barghuwata in 1058-9. The leadership of the Almoravides passed to Abu Bakr Ibn Umar and from then on the movement was divided into two parts: northern and southern. The northern branch under Abu Bakr's cousin, Yusuf Ibn Tashfin, conquered the Iberian peninsula, while the southern branch continued their jihad south of the Sahara. The prevailing story has been that in 1076, the Almoravides, Muslim warriors, crossed the Senegal River and conquered Ghana in the name of Islam, but some scholars argue against this version of events stating that the records of men writing in the 11th and 12th century did not mention a conquest. Mervyn Hiskette and Peter Clarke are among such scholars. According to Hiskette and Clarke, scholars have depended on the writings of Ibn Khaldun and al-Maqrizi who wrote in the 14th century rather than the writings of al-Zuhri who wrote in the early 12th century and never mentioned a conquest. Al-Zuhri, writes of cooperation between Ghana and the Almoravides. There is however, mention of the Almoravides waging jihad against other kingdoms of the area. As a matter of fact, Al-Zuhri's account details Ghana fighting one such kingdom alongside the Almoravides. The jihads of the Almoravides are the first example of wide-scale violent tactics aimed at religious expansion in the *Bilad as-Sudan.*[5]

Mali

The ancient Empire of Ghana waned in power and eventually was replaced by the Empire of Mali founded by Sunjata Keita (ca. 1234-55). Sunjata was Islamized as was his kingdom. The Keitas claim descent from Bilali Bunama who is considered to be the same Bilal Ibn Rahab who was among Muhammad's first converts. Bilal was an African slave from Ethiopia, who was the first Muslim muezzin, calling people for prayer. He was also a leading poet. In short, Bilal was among the early leaders of Islam. The claim of descent from Bilal reflects Mali's leaders understanding of the important role played by the first famous black Muslim in the history of early Islam This is evident of the presence of Islam in the region before the formation of the Empire of Mali in 1235.

According to Al-Bakri, a ruler of Mali was converted to Islam during a drought. The traditional priests had prayed for rain unsuccessfully. A Muslim guest of the king offered to pray for rain if the king promised to convert and have his people convert to Islam. The Muslim's prayer was successful so the ruler converted. Al-Bakri mentions that the commoners remained in their traditional religions.[6] This form of top-down conversion pattern was typical. With this type of conversion Islam becomes associated with the government and powerful people. As Sheikh Babou notes "the association of Muslim clerics with the business of government helped enhance the prestige of Islam and its expansion among the commoners."[7] Although Babou was writing about Islam among the West African states, the same observation rings true in all states of the Bilad al-Sudan where Islam was a feature of the royal court.

Malian society was rigidly hierarchical; therefore, the divisions between commoners and the nobility served as an obstacle and filter for the expansion of Islam. In this environment, retentions from the traditional religion persisted. Over time, however, a drive toward a more orthodox practice of Islam gave birth to a scholarly community that was respected throughout the Islamic world as well as the building of mosques and the institutionalization of Islam in Mali. This means Islam expanded slowly in Mali from an early core of believers over many years.

When Mansa Musa (1312-37), the most famous emperor of Mali, went on pilgrimage to Mecca in 1327, he impressed the Muslim world with a display of the fabulous wealth of Mali. With his generosity, Mansa Musa also attracted Muslim scholars, artisans, architects, and other skilled men and brought them to Mali. It was those artisans who helped Mansa Musa build some of the beautiful mosques in the Empire of Mali, including the elegant mosque in the city of Timbuktu. Mansa Musa's construction of an Afro-Islamic civilization base in his empire resulted from his famous pilgrimage or *hajj*.

While on *hajj*, Mansa Musa spent time in conversation with Islamic rulers and Islamic scholars. Al-Umari reports that Mansa Musa gave so much gold in the city of Cairo, Egypt, in 1327 that the price of gold was depressed for over a decade after his visit to Cairo. Al-Umari also reports that Mansa Musa made an impression as a very devout and sincere Muslim. One story recounts a custom for families to offer their beautiful girls to Musa as a gift when the girl came of age and Musa possessed these free-born girls as concubines contrary to Islamic law. Ibn Amir Hajib told Musa that it is wrong to live with free women without the benefit of marriage. Musa replied, "not even for kings?" Hajib responded in the negative. Musa replied, "By God, I did not know that! I hereby leave it and abandon it utterly."[8]

As stated above, Mansa Musa brought back artisans, architects, scholars, and other useful people and quickly began to construct centers of Islamic Civilization. Students were sent from Mali to other Muslim countries in North Africa and Egypt. In fact, Mansa Musa established hostels for students from Mali in Cairo. Those Malian students who graduated from the institution of higher learning in the Muslim countries returned to Mali, where they established Muslim schools, mosques and served as teachers, preachers, scholars, imams (prayer leaders), *qadis* (Muslim judges), interpreters and standard bearers of Islam. In fact, it was the Malian educated class that established endowed institutions of higher learning with their own libraries.

Timbuktu was one of the cities that flowered during the reign of Mansa Musa. During the 15th and 16th centuries, Timbuktu became the most famous bastion of Islamic learning in Western Africa.

As an expanding Empire, Mali brought Islam to surrounding areas and strengthened Islam in Muslim kingdoms. From what has transpired thus far, it can be said the Empire of Mali was an agent for the expansion of Islam in the region as well as a force for Islamic conformity. The same can be said for Songhai and most of the successor states in the region. The alliance of Islam and the state is an important aspect of Islamic expansion.

Songhai

Gao, the capital of Songhai, was one of the oldest towns in Western Africa. It was one of the areas where Islam spread during the 9th century. In fact, it has been claimed that Songhai had a Muslim king in the 9th century who transferred the capital from Kukiya to Gao where it remained up to the 15th century. Songhai was conquered by one of the generals of Mansa Musa and became a vassal state of Mali. Nevertheless, it was one of the first states to break away from the crumbling empire of Mali during the last quarter of the 14th century.

The empire of Songhai had an alliance with Islam, but there was a stiff competition for power between the monarchy and the scholarly community. Sonni Suleiman Mar led Songhai to independence from Mali in the late 14th century. However, Songhai was transformed into the biggest empire in Western Africa during the reign of Sonni Ali (1463-92). He was a warrior king, who conducted no less than 339 military campaigns. It was in the course of those campaigns that he captured the city of Timbuktu in 1472. Sunni Ali faced strong opposition from the scholarly community who had its base at Timbuktu. He persecuted some of the scholars of Timbuktu who he accused of consorting with the Tuaregs, his enemies. Sonni Ali had just conquered Timbuktu from the Tuaregs and his purging of their supporters could only be expected. History has since given him a bad name when it comes to Islam. Sonni Ali, however, has been credited with supporting mosques and Islamic learning. Like all rulers, however, he did not want the religious establishment undermining his authority. Sonni Ali was a nominal Muslim, however, and ran a country where the most educated and the wealthiest and the dominant part of the population were Muslims. His brutality toward his enemies, however, led to great disaffection, especially among the ulamma (scholarly community) of Timbuktu. Therefore, it was a sigh of relief for the scholarly community when Sunni Ali died in 1492.

Askia Muhammad took the kingdom from Sonni Ali's son Sonni Baru after Baru refused to declare himself a Muslim. Askia Muhammad's commitment to the expansion of Islam was unparalleled. He quickly asserted his status as a Muslim, made a celebrated pilgrimage, and took advice from the famed Tunisian scholar al-Maghili on how to run a Muslim state. According to some sources, he even made Islam the exclusive state religion, thereby outlawing the traditional African religions from which Sonni Ali had derived his power and influence.

Askia Muhammad grew old and blind and his sons took usurped power exiling him to an island in the Niger River. The consequent power struggle and instability weakened the state and made it easy for the sultan of Morocco to send in mercenaries and overrun the empire in 1592. The Moroccan invasion was debilitating for the state and Islam in the area as many of the scholars were taken in shackles back to Fez. The Islamic academies in Timbuktu suffered a great weakening that spread to the surrounding area. Songhai was already a state of a non-Muslim majority. A weakened Islamic establishment led to Islam losing ground in the area.

Jakhanke and the Unbelievers

With the fall of Songhai, a power vacuum existed in the Western Sudan. Smaller kingdoms rose in prominence and fell, but none of the size and power of Ghana, Mali, or Songhai. The progress of Islam, however, persisted in spite of the failure of Empire. The Jakhanke and other groups of mobile scholars were an alternate expansion agent to the previously mentioned war and state-sponsored Islam. The Jakhanke were a group of families led by Salim Suware from

Jahka (Diakha in the French eppelation) in Mali. They established a peaceful tradition of spreading Islam throughout the Western Sudan. Moving first to what is now Eastern Senegal in the kingdom of Bondu, Salim Suware and later his followers established villages all of which had at the center a mosque and several Qur'anic schools. The Jakhanke often fled warring situations in an attempt to stay peaceful.[9]

Salim Suware migrated early from Mali (sources are confused as to exactly when) to Senegambia. His followers came along and spread out in the area. Following the example of Suware, the Jakhanke upheld peaceful relations with their wider host societies and quietly practiced their religion. The natives began to convert to Islam, and with time the Jakhanke's method of keeping the peace proved successful and continued as a pattern throughout Senegambia. Lamin Sanneh's work on the Jakhanke brings light not only to their contribution to the expansion of Islam in the area but also to the peaceful aspect of Islamic conversion in sub-Saharan Africa. Scholars have concentrated on the violent jihads at the expense of the story of the Jakhanke and others who followed their example. Thus, when Sheikh Ahmadou Bamba, Limamou Laye, and El Hajj Malik Sy adopt a non-confrontational stance to the French government, they were not establishing a new response to Islam under a nonbelieving government. On the contrary, they were resorting to the practice typified under the tutelage of Salim Suware.

Senegambia

Senegambia had a strong Islamic influence that dated from the 9th century. Like many other places, it was also state sponsored in certain parts of the region. In other areas, it was due solely to the activities of the Jakhanke and the Malinke trading group, the Joola. Over the centuries, Islam was the religion of a select elite and of the court. However, Islam became an important counterpoint to the political oppression of the court as independent religious leaders took in runaway slaves and looked forward to an Islamic government. Waves of violent jihadist expression weakened the states, emboldened generations of Islamic leaders, and created a situation ripe and ready for European conquest.

The major political unit of Senegambia, the Jolof Empire, was conquered by the Empire of Mali in the mid-13th century and remained a vassal state until the mid-14th century.[10] In 1549, Koli Tengella came from Songhai where the emperor had killed his father for trying to assert independence and conquered Fouta Toro establishing the Denianke dynasty.[11] While building his empire and expanding its borders, Tengella also killed the Emperor of Jolof and took Takhrur. The ruling family of Jolof subsequently experienced prolonged strife, which intensified instability leading to the vassal states breaking away and declaring their independence. The Jolof Empire was then divided into five kingdoms: Cayor, Waalo, Jolof, Bawol, and Sine-Saluum. Waalo, being in proximity to the Arabized Moors, were the recipients of an already old Islamic influence. The Serer kingdom of Sine-Saluum effectively resisted Islam until the late 19th century, and today many Serer people are either Christians or traditionalists.

In Cayor, Jolof, and Bawol, Islam continued to progress gradually.[12] Islam in the region would undergo successive waves of reform usually in the form of a violent jihad. Most scholars have chronicled these violent episodes crediting them with the proper Islamization of the region. The supposition is that Islam did not experience widespread conversions until the 19th century. Paul Marty's work *Islam au Senegal* as well as his other works on Islam in French Africa are all built on the assumption that first Islam *noir* is not as good as Islam. The early French colonial officials, relying on reports from their scholars such as Paul Marty, among others, accepted this idea and shared it with the French colonial office, thus it was a basis of French policy in dealing with Muslims in their sub-Saharan African colonies. This argument assumes two things: the Islam that predates the 19th century was not 'real' Islam and violence was the principle vehicle for the expansion of Islam in the region. In recent times, a reassessment of this theory has come forth from scholars such as David Robinson who describes the process of Islamization occurring simultaneously with the process of Africanization of Islam.[13] This reassessment of the facts also speaks to the truth about the portability of Islam. There is no monolithic

Islam. Like any other portable religious belief system, Islam adapts to fit the various cultural superstructures where it spread. Thus, as Eunice Charles argues, the Islam *noir* of Sub-Saharan Africa is no less Islam than the Christianity of Western Europe (which is greatly different from the original Middle Eastern Christianity) is any less Christian.

Starting with the conversion of Njaanjaan Njaay, the founder of the Jolof Empire, a symbiotic, though often adverse, relationship developed between Islam and the noble families throughout Waalo, Jolof, Cayor, and Bawol. As was the case with the Ghana Empire, the Muslims were needed for their ability to write and secondly, and sometimes more importantly, their spiritual stature in regards to prayer requests and the manufacture of amulets and charms. Certain Muslims were granted lands through their service as advisors and amulet makers. The Muslims built prosperous villages and attracted converts from runaway slaves and peasants who wanted protection from capture and enslavement by the *ceddo,* royal slave military caste who often resorted to capturing peasants and exchanging them for European goods. These converts provided labor, which increased wealth and influence for the Muslim villages. Thus Islamic leaders became important potential allies for noble families. The Islamic leaders also benefited from these alliances with increased political power as well as familial contacts through marriages.[14]

In this way Islam had penetrated Senegambian society but the lax practices of the nobles coupled with the fact that Islamic leaders of the court did not want to endanger their influential positions by preaching against the nobles and monarch kept this penetration at a relatively surface level. Muslim men shaved their heads while the nobles grew their hair long. Some nobles paid their marabouts (Muslim holy man) to fast and pray for them. Marabouts also continued to make amulets, charms, and work magic for the rulers and nobles for monetary gain contrary to the laws of Islam.[15]

The result was an easy cohabitation of Islam and traditional religious practices. European observers said this Islam was not pure Islam due to the "ignorance of those who introduced it . . . and the nature of those who embraced it."[16] The Europeans spoke out of their racist ignorance, but many Islamic leaders in the region saw the lax Islam as a threat to the faith. At least this is what Islamic combatants claimed when they warred in the name of Islam in order to acquire temporal power.

The Greater Jihad and the Lesser Jihad

There is a sometimes-discredited Hadith, which recounts the Prophet Mohammad telling his followers after a war, "We have returned from the lesser jihad (*jihad al-asghar*) to the greater jihad (*jihad al-akbar*)." He goes on to describe *jihad al-akbar* as "the struggle against oneself."[17] The concept of jihad al-asghar is not foreign to Islam in any part of the world. Throughout the history of Islam in the Western Sudan, there has been violent jihad. As mentioned above, Abdallah ibn Yasin held violent jihad as a viable means of expanding Islam. Jihad al-Akbar is also present in the policies of Salim Suware and the Jakhanke with their rather controversial policy of tolerating a non-Islamic leader and society while gradually gaining converts. These two brands of jihad continued to coexist as active agents of Islamic expansion in Senegambia and beyond. The battle was never lost on any Muslims regardless of where they were in Western Sudan or whichever type of jihad to which they subscribed.

The first of such combatants was Nasr al-Din, a Muslim cleric from one of the major *zwaya*, which is the collective name for the clerical tribes of North Africa who facilitated the spread of Islam in the Western Sudan. Nasr al-Din began the violent phase of his mission around 1673 and was quickly crushed in 1677. The significance of this event to our discussion is Nasr al-Din's reason for going to war and the extent of his uprising.[18]

Nasr al-Din preached for many years and built a considerable following before he decided to strike out against the nominal Muslims in the vicinity. More pointedly, he wanted to spearhead an Islamic Revival that would foster a central Islamic government thereby superseding the existing divisions. Al-Din's vision was to be the successor to the caliphs of the earlier stages, which also meant that he would have all temporal and spiritual powers vis-a-vis the surrounding people. His first step was to send out an appeal to recognize his authority. He followed up with emissaries. He reached out to Jolof, Waalo, Cayor, and Fouta Toro. First it was an innocent message to submit to God, but later it developed into a call to submit to al-Din's authority. Although unsuccessful, Nasr al-Din's revolt set a precedence that was repeated over the next two centuries.[19]

Malik Sy created the Islamic state of Bondu around 1696. Some scholars have treated this event as a jihad while others don't define but assume it as a consequence of Nasr al-Din's jihad.[20] Recently a more careful study of the oral and written sources has netted a different interpretation. Michael Gomez in his study of Bondu characterizes the whole episode as a matter of state development where Islam was present but not a major organizing factor. Andrew Clark echoes these views.[21] The resulting state was primarily secular with Muslim citizens, thus Bondu was the exception to the pattern of jihad that continued to explode after Nasr al-Din's jihad.

In Fouta Jallon, Alfa Karamoko (also known as Musa Ibrahim and Alfa Ibrahim Sembegu) launched a jihad against the Jalonke rulers of the area in the 1720's. The Alfa Karamoko was a Fulani who, thanks to Koli Tengella's state building of the 15th century, came to settle in Fouta Jallon. By the 18th century, there were considerable numbers and they naturally conflicted with the Jalonke, Susu, and Mandingo who were already settled in the region. The pastoralist Fulani conflicted with the farming Jalonke, Susu, and Mandingo. Alfa Karamoko used Islam as a unifying factor for the Fulani, and they fought a successful jihad that eventually crumbled into two camps after Alfa Karamoko's death. One group was devout Muslims, and the other group was more into the political advantages of conquest.

In 1776, the Denianke dynasty of Fouta Toro (presently part of Senegal) was overthrown in the jihad of Suleiman Bal. Nasr al-Din's jihad had greatly destabilized the Denianke dynasty and the Trarza Moors were a constant threat to the independence of Fouta Toro. Suleiman Bal rose and gathered a group of faithful fighters around him in order to fend off the threat and restore order. In doing so, he overthrew the now inept Denianke (who, at the founding of the dynasty, were celebrated as Muslim rulers in the Arabic sources), and died in a battle against the Trarza Moors. Abd al-Qadir took the head of the new Islamic state after being elected 'almamy' (al-imam), which is literally translated from the Arabic as 'leader of the prayer.' In Fouta Toro, almamy became the title of the leader of the government. Abd al-Qadir defeated the Trarza Moors and spread the jihad to Bondu and Cayor about which we will discuss more below.

Cayor, the most powerful former vassal of Jolof, experienced two major Islamic uprisings led by orthodox marabouts, holy men, who commanded large armies. The first rebellion was part of Nasr al-Din's wider rebellion and lasted from 1673-4 and the second one took place in 1795. Both of these rebellions were put down with much effort, but the fact that they took place shows two things. First, the Europeans were wrong about ignorance of Muslims in Senegambia. Secondly, the separation between practiced Islam and orthodox Islam was visibly a problem for elements of the Islamic community.[22]

Marabouts fleeing the wrath of the dameel (king) Latsukaabe Ngone Joop of Cayor in 1795 ran southwest and found refuge among the Lebu. The Maraboutic family that established their suzerainty over the Lebu is the Joop family. Dial Joop was the first of these leaders. The Joop family settled among the Lebu and established an Islamic theocracy after having led the Lebu in a successful rebellion against the Kingdom of Cayor. There has been considerable dispute over whether the Joop established a republic or a kingdom.[23] There definitely were traces of both forms of government present in the Lebu political organization, but assigning a foreign label to the government is irrelevant to real observation and, for the purpose of this study, a waste of time. Thus it is sufficient for us to say that the Lebu had a well-organized government that defies an appropriate Western label. We will discuss this further in the next chapter.

Four Jihads in 19th Century Senegambia 1869-86

The region of Senegambia had four major leaders with political aspirations that ended in violent jihad. The first jihad in this series is that of El-Hajj Omar Tall. El-Hajj Omar took the title El-Hajj or pilgrim after returning from Mecca in 1838. He came as the newly appointed caliph of the Tijaniyya Brotherhood for the Western Sudan and installed himself in present-day Guinea. Within a decade, he had begun establishing politico-religious units first in present-day Guinea and then in present-day Mali.

He was of the Tukeleur tribe, from which came the foot soldiers of Islamic propagation in the Western Sudan. Tall's jihad set off a chain of events that ended in full-scale French conquest. The jihad of El Hajj Omar Tall upset the peace and hindered trade. The French response was slow and hesitant, but eventually the decisive action was a dismantling of the Senegambian states.

El-Hajj Omar married the daughter of Sultan Mohammed Bello of Hausaland. Afterwards El-Hajj Omar moved to Fouta Jallon. In 1848, he started his jihad from the small Islamic theocracy that he had formed in Dinguiraye. He moved north and conquered the Bambara of Nioro and Kaarta. In 1861, he conquered the Bambara kingdom of Segu (present day Mali). In 1862, he violated the sacred *umma* (Muslim community) by attacking the Islamic state Hamdullahi. He conquered Hamdullahi, but disappeared in the Bandiagara Hills in 1864. One of the goals of El-Hajj Omar's struggle was the elimination of the French from the area.[24]

In 1861, a disciple of El-Hajj Omar, Maba Jakhou Ba, invaded the province of Rip in the kingdom of Saloum. Later in 1864 Maba conquered all of Saloum and began to wage war on all the states in the Senegambia region. In violation of a treaty with the French, Maba invaded Jolof and then Cayor. While in Jolof, he advised all Muslims who were capable to go to Saloum in order to escape hurt or harm from the ensuing war or retaliation from their leaders. Saloum at this time was full of Islamic clerics, jurists, and scholars from all over the region. For a brief period the kingdom rivaled the scholastic atmosphere of medieval Timbuktu. Exiled candidate for the throne of Cayor, Lat-Joor Latyr Ngone Joop fled to Saloum and was among those seeking Momar Antasali's advice.

Lat-Dior's story will lead us into the third jihad in the series. Lat-Joor's problems began when the dameel Birama Ngoné Latyr died in 1859. The *dameels* of Cayor were chosen by a supreme executive council from among major contenders. The candidates waged a campaign of political influence and, sometimes, physical warfare. Lat-Joor was a contender for the throne after the death of Birama Ngoné Latyr. The supreme executive council asked for a suggestion from the French governor Faidherbe. Faidherbe had already planned to conquer Cayor and went about it in a calculating fashion. He chose Makodu Kumba Joof. Makodu tried to reoccupy the land that the French had taken during the reign of Birama Ngoné Latyr. The French invaded Cayor in January of 1861 and tried to force a treaty on Makodu. The treaty called for Makodu to let the French take possession of the disputed provinces. Makodu refused. In March and May of 1861, the French again invaded Cayor, defeated Makodu, and installed Majojo on the throne.

Lat-Dior and his forces fought and won against Majojo and the French in 1862. With the aid of the French, Majojo defeated Lat-Joor and drove him and his followers out of Cayor. The French then instituted a veritable puppet government. In order to not incite the wrath of Maba and his forces, the French sought and acquired a treaty with Maba in which Maba promised the safety of Senegalese troops while in Saloum and the respect of the French protectorate of Jolof, Cayor, Bawol, and the Serer kingdom of Siin. In exchange Faidherbe agreed to recognize Maba's government in Saloum. At the same time, Faidherbe suggested to the English governor a Franco-English alliance to eliminate Maba. It was not long before the French saw that their government with Majojo was ineffective. On January 17, 1865, Faidherbe deposed Majojo and annexed Cayor dividing it into five provinces. As stated above, Lat-Joor had fled to Saloum.

Lat-Dior concreted an alliance with Maba by accepting Islam or rather renewing his faith. Maba strengthened himself with Lat-Dior's troops, and Lat-Dior rested in the hope that Maba would help him regain Cayor. In collaboration, the two did come to propagate their pro-Islamic and anticolonial message throughout Senegambia. However, on July 28, 1867, Maba invaded Siine. The Buurba Siine and his French allies defeated Maba, and he died in heat of the battle.

The leader of Fouta Toro, Sheikh Ahmadu Ba, popularly known as Ahmadou Sheku, began to recruit people for his jihad at this time. He also made overtures to Lat-Joor. Fearing an alliance between Lat-Joor and Ahmadou Sheku, the new French governor of Senegal, Pinet-Laprade invited Lat-Dior to move with his family back to Cayor and become the chief of Lat-Dior's natal province of Guet. Pinet-Laprade outlined his stipulations in a letter to Lat-Dior. "You command the country under my orders. The people of Guet pay the personal tax to the French government. You promise not to engage in a war without my ordering it."[25]

Ahmadou Sheku continued to rally many to his cause by preaching that God was punishing the people with the economic problems, famine, and yellow fever epidemic that had swept the region. People converted *en masse* because they were tired of French aggression, which could easily be connected to the problems of the region. The French invasion of Cayor during the reign of Makodu brought destruction to the crops. The continued fighting between Lat-Joor and Majojo/French alliance furthered the destruction. With this in mind, the people's acceptance of Ahmadou Sheku's message is not confusing.

Lat-Joor allied with Ahmadou Sheku and the French fought them both. Pinet-Laprade died of cholera in August of 1869. His replacement, Valère, saw the mess that Cayor had become and the disastrous effect it had on commerce. In an attempt to reestablish order in Cayor and destroy the Lat-Dior/Ahmadou Sheku alliance, Valere, in 1871, invited Lat-Joor to come and rule Cayor again.

Eventually, the alliance between Lat-Dior and Ahmadou Sheku fell apart, which was part of Valere's plan. When he signed the treaty with the French on January 12, 1871, Lat-Joor began to distance himself from Ahmadou Sheku. In 1870, Lat-Joor had even cleared the border of Cayor allowing the French to come into Fouta Toro and attack the supporters of Ahmadou Sheku. After Lat-Joor took power, Ahmadou Sheku continued to exercise his authority through his representatives in the Islamic provinces of Cayor. The definitive break, however, came when Lat-Joor attacked Ce Yasin Galo Gano, the tegne, king, of Bawol. Lat-Joor wanted to unite Cayor and Bawol by occupying both thrones. When the council of Bawol elected Ce Yasin Galo Gano, Lat-Joor attacked Bawol. Ahmadou Sheku, who had taken over Jolof, opposed this because he had his own plans for Bawol where he had many followers. The French stood by and let this seed of discord grow between the two leaders. When Ahmadou Sheku invaded Cayor in 1874, Lat-Joor and the French combined forces on February 11, 1876 at the battle of Samba Sajo, when they defeated and killed the marabout and his closest disciples.

In 1885, El Hajj Muhammad Al-Amin Demba Dibassi, more popularly known as Mamadu Lamin, returned to Senegambia after many years spent traveling, seven of which in Mecca. He wanted to wage violent jihad against the people of Gamel. Mamadu Lamin spent his childhood in Bondu. The oral sources offer different versions for his grudge against the people. One version says that Mamadu Lamine and his mother were captured in a slave raid by the people of Gamel where his mother died before she could be ransomed. Another version recounts Mamadou Lamine alone being captured on a failed raid of Gamel. Whatever the case, this supposed jihad was personal. Mamadu Lamine asked Bokar Saada Sy, the ruler of Bondu, for permission to cross Bondu in order to wage war against Gamel. Bokar Saada refused and died shortly thereafter. Mamadu Lamine took advantage of the Bundunke civil strife that followed Bokar Saada's death and invaded Bondu. In the spring of 1886, Mamadu Lamine conquered Bondu and established his capitol at Jana about 200 km southwest of the French trading post of Bakel. The bulk of French forces were engaged in a war with Samory Toure to the south of Bondu. Some members of the ousted Sissibe Dynasty sought French aid. In late 1886 the French and their Sissibe allies drove Mamadu Lamine out of Bondu. He was captured and killed in December 1887 in the upper Gambia region. This ended the last jihad in the series and really opened the door for full French conquest, for at this point, with the goal of protecting their trading interests, the French had entered so intimately into the political affairs of the surrounding kingdoms and gained experience governing Africans of the interior.[26]

In addition to these religious leaders was the already mentioned *dameel* (king) of Cayor, Lat-Joor Ngoné Latyr Joop, who fought and betrayed his fellow natives and the French at varying times in order to keep his personal power. Lat-Joor used Islam to identify with various Islamic leaders, but he sided with the French against the Brak of Waalo. His behavior was not out of the ordinary and portrays the principle of power that dominates most rulers, i.e. hold on to power at all costs.

Can we interpret his actions and those of other rulers as an indication of a weak Islam? No. Lat-Joor and the other Wolof sovereigns were concerned with the maintenance of their power. Their predecessors had successfully found a common ground with a steadily proliferating Islam and a stoutly defiant traditional religious establishment, thereby successfully avoiding destruction of their power. Lat-Joor and his contemporaries, however, were not prepared for the colonial onslaught. Unlike Menelik II of Ethiopia, they did not understand the broader global issues into which their existence had been pushed. They could not conceive of a new global order, much less their diminished position in it. Thus, the French colonialists armed with the assumption of their own supremacy (their greatest weapon) along with superior weaponry and the aid of African allies dispossessed Lat-Joor and his contemporaries of the erroneous notion that it was 'business as usual.' That lesson cost them their kingdoms and, in some cases, their lives.

El-Hajj Omar's jihad seems to have strong political goals. Why else would he attack another conservative Islamic state? El-Hajj Omar, however, did create a state that survived him until the French firmly rooted their hegemony. Before he died, he established cohesion in his government through his appointment of his sons as leaders of the conquered regions and the unifying factor of Islam.

Maba's jihad also had strong political goals. Maba's invasion of Jolof and Cayor can easily be justified because of the lax Islam of the leaders in these kingdoms. Maba's jihad failed, however, because of his zealous concentration on destroying those kingdoms that would not succumb to him. Serigne Bachirou evaluates Maba as a good Muslim who was not wise enough to rule effectively. Maba's lack of wisdom translated into a lack of cohesion in his government and more importantly a lack of a clear visible goal. Of course like all the others, Maba had the larger goal of Dar-al-Islam. He, however, should have had a more concrete and viable goal such as maintaining his grip on Saloum at the risk of abandoning his ambitions in Siine, Jolof, and Cayor.

Ahmadou Sheku's jihad was as much (if not more) anti-French as it was religious. In his preaching, he very plainly advocated turning against the French. Of course this message is one that had developed over the years with each successive jihad in the region and the increasingly aggressive French diplomacy. Therefore, he quickly found an audience in those who had suffered famine and disease because of

French invasions. This type of jihad will be seen a century later in the United States led by Elijah Muhammad, and in both cases, the result is a high convert rate. The major difference, however, is that Elijah Muhammad's jihad was an unarmed and relatively nonviolent affair whereas Ahmadou Sheku's jihad was very violent. Elijah Muhammad's converts became Muslim without terribly upsetting the society. On the contrary, members of the Nation of Islam are often more law-abiding, cleaner, and more community oriented than before their conversion, whereas the converts to Ahmadou Sheku's jihad were bent on turning the society on its head. Why did Ahmadou Sheku's jihad fail? His success depended on the cooperation of those, such as Lat-Dior, whose goals were not the same as his. When Lat-Dior reached his goal, he had no further use for Ahmadou Sheku. The French had no use for either and thus used Lat-Dior to hasten the end of Ahmadou Sheku, because like El-Hajj Omar and Maba before him, Ahmadou Sheku and his organization could not coexist with French colonization.

The colonial powers had no conflict with Islam per se. The French actually restricted the missionary activities of Catholics in their Islamic possessions citing concern at upsetting Muslim populations. The secular European states did not seek to impede one religion or another in Senegambia. There was a fear of Islamic militancy. Reeling from the fight with El Hajj Umar, Maba Jakhou Ba, Mamadu Lamine, and others, the French and the British were wary of any individual gathering large crowds around him. This paranoia translated into political oppression. Describing French policies Khadim Mbacke cites the French regulation of Islamic schools in St. Louis. The policies seem nothing beyond the norm for anyone living in a modern state. Muslims of late 19th century St. Louis, and obviously Mbacke, took offense to the state regulating education. Mbacke, however, makes a stronger case for his argument of French suppression of Islam when he describes how colonial authorities restricted the number of those allowed to do the hajj, restricted the import of books from the Islamic Holy Land, restricted contact between Senegalese Muslims and Muslims outside of French domain, and killed or arrested Islamic scholars.[27]

Mbacke's indictment of the French comes at the end of his chapter dealing with the Tijanis where he criticizes El Hajj Malik Sy's cooperation with the French. He then launches into praise of Sheikh Ahmadou Bamba Mbacke. Sheikh Ahamadu Bamba is quoted as having said "I know that Allah sent the toubab in order to bring peace to the country" when Lat-Joor asked him to join in fighting against the French.[28] Sheikh Ahamdu Bamba also cooperated with the French after his second exile. The French even offered him an award. Thus Mbacke's characterization of the whole ordeal is confusing at best. The question before us then, is "did the French and/or British wage a war against Islam?" The answer is no. Did French and/or British attack Islamic institutions in their path to conquest and domination? Of course they did. It was not a matter of which religion. The French brutally beat Christian leader William Wade Harris and his evangelistic team resulting in the death of one of his singers.[29] The British also fought the preachers in Sierra Leone. One governor of Freetown charged a preacher with "using the Holy Spirit as an excuse to cloak political effrontery."[30] The European colonizers simply desired to establish and spread their hegemony and crush any threat (real, perceived, or even suspected) to their efforts.

Islam in Senegal

During and after the French conquest, the Islam that developed in the Western Sudan was sufist and more pointedly maraboutic. As stated above the progress of Islam cannot be seen through the prism of European colonization. Islam and European colonization were two historical phenomenon who progressed on a parallel linear and eventually intersected at the decomposition of the precolonial states. The forces pushing for a more orthodox Islam met resistance from the royal courts of Senegambia all of which received the validation of their political authority from the pre-Islamic socioreligious order. Though most monarchs were at least nominally Muslims, pre-Islamic traditional religious practices persisted. Most historians assert in concert that large-scale conversion to Islam occurred on the eve of and during colonization, maintaining that only a minority of the population considered themselves Muslim. Though many historians offer this as fact, no proof is shown. In a region that had been acquainted with Islam since the 9th century and peaceful as well as violent proselytizing emissaries fanned throughout the region, it is hard to reconcile the assertion that after more than eight centuries, Muslims remained in the minority. The proliferation of jihads with the purpose of perfecting Islam should be evidence enough of at least a syncretic version of Islam being pervasive among the populations of Senegambia.

Sufism

Sufism is an articulation of Islam that began in Basra in present-day Iraq. It was seen as a challenge to the power of the *ulama* as well as the political powers. Repression was not successful and Sufism ultimately proliferated and spread throughout the Islamic world. Sufism became the most successful vehicle of Islamization at the frontiers of Islam. Jamil Abun-Nasr argues that the success of Sufism lies in its use of spiritual authority vested in the leaders of each tariqa. Initially the caliphs were to fill Muhammad's shoes as both spiritual and temporal power. Over time, according to Abun-Nasr, they failed in their roles as religious authorities as their lifestyles often contradicted the religion. With no clergy or prophets in place, the leaders of turuq filled the void.[31]

Sufism also appeals to many pre-Islamic cultures because of the concentration on acquiring esoteric knowledge. Each tariqa has a *wird* or combination of religious sayings used in prayer and meditation. Sufis also practice *dhikr* or repetitions of the names and attributes of the Divine in order to get closer to Him and purify the soul of the adherent. Renouncing the world and submission to a sheikh are also major tenets of all Sufi turuq. The sheikh is authorized to give the *wird* to adherents but only after they have shown themselves worthy. Study of the Quran is essential to this process, but Sufism places a greater emphasis on the esoteric understanding of the Quran and all things. This approach appeals to African Spirituality.

I define African Spirituality as a preoccupation with the esoteric and all things spiritual emanating from a universal worldview that there is a spirit world that is parallel to the physical world. These two worlds intersect a critical junctures, for example, in dreams, at birth, at death, in prayer, visions, meditation, etc. The strength of the traditional priests/priestess was his/her ability to navigate between the two worlds and to make sense of others' experiences with the spirit world. Primary to the priests'/priestesses' ability was the use of their knowledge to effect change in the physical world, that is, return of a lost loved one, healing of the sick, and other miracles that lay outside the ability of the average person in the physical world. The above description could be applied to almost any indigenous traditional religion throughout the world. In African Spirituality, however, there is a persistent belief that the spirit and physical world are in constant flux with the contact between the two exceeding beyond the acknowledged critical junctures. For example, one's ancestors are always present in all activities watching and acting even though it is out of the view of the physical eye.

Senegalese Islam

As Christianity spreads across Africa, we see a proliferation of Pentecostal and charismatic churches because these expressions of Christian experience appeal to African Spirituality. In much the same way Sufism spoke to African Spirituality and the conversation continues. Thus, Islam underwent a marked change towards the end of the precolonial era. It became indigenized through the vehicle of Sufism, particularly when two indigenous Sufi turuq sprung to life. In modern Senegal, there are four major Sufi turuq (plural of Arabic tariqa) to which the majority of Senegalese Muslims claim membership. The first is the Qadriyya that originated in Baghdad from the teachings of Abd al-Qadir al-Jilani in ca. 1133 and spread to sub-Saharan Africa in the 18th century. The Quadiriyya does not have organizational or doctrinal unity as does other Sufi turuq. Emanating from the teachings of popularity of al-Jilani and the organizational skills of his son, the Quadiriyya spread throughout the Muslim world and was on the frontline of Islamic expansion from present-day Mauritania into Senegambia.

The next one is the Tijaniyya, which began as a result of the teachings of the Algerian marabout Ahmad al-Tijani who proclaimed that he was the Imam of the prophet and established a rule of exclusivity among his followers. As the prophet Muhammad did with Islam, al-Tijani attempted to cap the growing field of sufi organizations with his proclamation. As Imam of the prophet, he successfully attached himself and his authority to the prophet citing a vision in which he saw Muhammad and was commissioned to establish a unique tariqa. The adherents to the Tijaniyya are forbidden to practice the wird of another sect. Al-Tijani's teachings came to Senegambia, which was dominated by the Qadiriyya sect. Under the auspices of El-Hajj Umar Tall and later El-Hajj Malik Sy, and Abd Allah Niasse the Tijaniyya spread throughout Senegambia.

The indigenization of Islam in Senegal began in earnest with Sheikh Ahmadou Bamba Mbacke proclaiming himself *khadim rassul*, or servant of the prophet Muhammad, and founding his tariqa, the Muridiyya. His teaching style was more palatable to the average Senegalese peasant because he emphasized work along with study. Upon arriving in one of his compound, the adherent was given an aptitude test of sorts. If it was found that the adherent was better suited for farm work, his time was split between work in the fields and learning the Quran and basics of the religion. Others with more of a scholastic aptitude were taught the Quran as well as more advanced areas of Islamic knowledge. Sheikh Ahmadou Bamba's idea was that religious education should be life-long with the ultimate idea of improving the adherent's spiritual life and demeanor.

The Muridiyya grew quickly and attracted the negative attention of the French who were looking to prevent any more violent episodes. Sheikh Ahmadou Bamba was eventually arrested and exiled twice (once in 1895 and again in 1903). His tariqa continued to grow and prosper during his exile and continues to expand. It is the second largest tariqa in modern-day Senegal with approximately 33% of the Senegalese Muslim population claiming membership. Because of the migrant Senegalese workers in European and North American cities, the Muridiyya has reached beyond Africa and claims American and European adherents leading to the translation of Sheikh Ahmadou Bamba's writings into French and English.

Muride success cannot be explained only with a more culturally attuned pedagogy. Sheikh Ahmadou Bamba Mbacke offered his followers something more concrete. His tariqa was an adequate answer to the social, political, and economic upheavals that had accelerated during the last decades of the 19th century. These upheavals cannot be attributed to colonization solely. The pursuit of luxury goods and territory coupled with the introduction of firearms and the European/American greed for slaves exacerbated existing divisions on the Senegambian sociopolitical scene leading to more than three centuries of intermittent warfare and political decay that culminated in European colonization. Previous Muslim leaders had added to the strife with violent jihads. Sheikh Ahmadu Bamba shunned violent jihad and presented a third alternative to those who thought they could only sellout to the French or fight. Echoing the example of Salim Suware and the Jakhanke, Sheikh Ahmadu Bamba's option was to pursue the religion with indifference and often in spite of the political scenery.

Most importantly, Sheikh Ahmadou Bamba's popularity involved his spiritual credentials. The average Senegalese was illiterate and could only recite enough of the Qur'an to complete his prayers, if any at all. Operating under their worldview of authority equating patronage, a spiritual leader was only as good as his ability to do something. In other words, if a spiritual leader could not use his esoteric knowledge to affect change in the physical world, he was of no use to anyone. Sheikh Ahmadou Bamba is credited with many healings, prosperity, etc. His prayers were counted among the most effective. His *baraka* was counted especially potent. Just being close to such a potent marabout netted physical rewards for the adherent. Giving him a gift entitled the giver to the benefits of his spiritual power. In other words, the people flocked to Sheikh Ahmadou Bamba Mbacke because, in the words of the classic Aretha Franklin song, he gave them something they could feel.

He was born into a family steeped in Islamic devotion and scholarship. His father, Mohammad ibn Habib el Allah Mbacké, was a great Islamic jurist and teacher. His mother was Maryam Boussou whose family is also in the hierarchy of Senegalese Islamic families. Maryam Bousso was called Diaratouallah or neighbor of God. This name is meant to illustrate her closeness to God through her constant devotion. She prayed the five times a day in accordance with Islamic practices, but she also prayed often during the night. She took great pains to instill piety in her children. As a young child Cheikh Ahmadou Bamba followed her example and continued it throughout his lifetime.[32]

Added to this lifetime of near constant prayer was the traditional Islamic education. While Cheikh Ahmadou Bamba was still rather young, his father sent him to Jolof to study under his maternal great-uncle, Mbacké Ndoumbé until he reached the age to begin his Koranic studies. While in Jolof, he actually began a study of the Koran. Mbacké Nboumbé died suddenly while copying the Koran and Cheikh Ahmadou Bamba then went to his maternal uncle Muhammad Bousso.

Cheikh Ahmadou Bamba came into manhood during the strife of Maba. By the time he came to Patar to live with his father, he was already teaching. His father eventually moved to Mbacké-Cayor where he died in 1883. Cheikh Ahmadou Bamba continued his teaching and studying. He followed the conventional practice of the time in his education. This consisted of going to masters, living with and learning from them, and receiving a diploma, which constituted a license to teach that particular subject. Cheikh Ahmadou Bamba was educated in this manner. He studied the Qur'an, theology, literature, lexicography, philology, composition/poetry, and logic. In 1886, he took the name Khadim er Rassul (servant of the prophet). After studying under many masters, he decided that God was his only master, thereby establishing his authority and his mystic "voice."

After acquiring several diplomas, Cheikh Ahmadou Bamba established himself in Cayor and abandoned himself to an ascetic life of teaching and preaching. He was not, however, alone. He quickly developed a reputation as a pious and spiritually powerful man. This reputation spread far and wide in the Senegambia region and beyond. Consequently, people of all walks of life flocked to him before and especially after the death of his father. He exhibited early that he had no interest in anything other than his religious activities. When Albuuri Ndiaye was under assault from the French, he approached Cheikh Ahmadou Bamba for aid. According to the oral tradition the conversation went as such: Albuuri Ndiaye told Cheikh Ahmadou Bamba, "I will fight against the toubab[33] who don't pray and I will be your Ali-Samba." Cheikh Ahmadou Bamba then responded, "I know that Allah sent the toubab in order to bring peace to the country. You will get men killed for nothing whereas if they live they will convert to Islam. If however you are bent on fighting, you will find in the East a warrior marabout (El-Hajj Omar Tall). You only have to join up with him.[34]

While Cheikh Ahmadou Bamba was living with his father and teaching, Samba Laobé, the last dameel of Cayor, came and asked if Cheikh Ahmadou Bamba would come and be his cadi. The Cheikh forced him to wait until he had finished with his students for the day. He then met the dameel outside of his father's house and gave him his response, "it is not possible for me to leave my students who have come to learn the precepts of the religion. Far from me is that idea." Samba Laobé then gave him a horse but there were two Muslims who had loaned money to the dameel, and they wanted their money. The Cheikh sold the horse and repaid the men their money.

These two stories illustrate Cheikh Ahmadou Bamba's abandon to his religious activities and his boldness before secular leaders. As his own jihad took shape and form, he consistently illustrated a total concentration on the "greater jihad." This jihad consisted of work and devotion. Cheikh Ahmadou Bamba is quoted as having said, "Work as if you will live forever, and pray as if you will die tomorrow." This was at the heart of his theology. After his father's death and the end of his education, Cheikh Ahmadou Bamba attracted talibes (students) from all over the region as well as visits from other noted religious figures. When a talibe arrived, either the Cheikh or his lieutenants administered a sort of aptitude test. According to the results, a student entered either a program of basic religious instruction as well as work in the fields or a program of reading and writing in Arabic and learning the Koran and the religious sciences.[35]

Among the students of the Cheikh were the royal and noble families of the Senegambia region. Cheikh Ahmadou Bamba also held ties with Saer Mati, the son of Maba Jakhou Ba. Saer Mati had installed himself in present-day Gambia and refused to recognized French authority. The Cheikh's constant flow of visitors and his large number of talibes caused many local chiefs to fear the Cheikh's encroaching on their authority. These chiefs then went to complain to the French. Among these was the Buur Njambuur.

Adding to the problem was the Cheikh's constant moving. The Cheikh's son, Serigne Bachirou, said the Cheikh only wanted privacy to pursue his religious activities.[36] The French saw him moving constantly into regions where the traditional power was destroyed and assumed that he wanted to find a power vacuum to establish political authority. There is no concrete historical evidence to support either explanation because one can never know for sure what another thinks. However, the fact that the Cheikh never tried to set up a government nor armed his followers makes it possible to assume that Serigne Bachirou is accurate.

Whatever the case, the French government assumed that the Cheikh was up to no good. When the Cheikh moved into the Lower Ferlo, the French became particularly alarmed and set up close surveillance. The Lower Ferlo is halfway between the Senegal and Gambia rivers as well as being an equal distance from Jolof, Cayor, and Bawol. The memory of El-Hajj Omar, Maba, and Ahmadou Sheku, as well as the menace of Saer Mati fueled the fear of the French and drove them to eventually exile Cheikh Ahmadou Bamba on 21 September 1895.

From 1895 to 1903, the Cheikh was exiled to Gabon. Again from 1903 to 1907, he was exiled to Mauritania. During both exiles, the Mourride Brotherhood did not fall away. To understand the reasons for this, it is necessary now to examine the differences between the previous jihads in the region and that of Cheikh Ahmadou Bamba.

Cheikh Ahmadou Bamba never organized a group of armed men. The French accused him of it, but they themselves found no proof of it. Some of his followers did commit acts of violence, but he quickly verbally chastised them and distanced himself from them. Therefore, the most obvious difference between the jihad of Cheikh Ahmadou Bamba and those of El-Hajj Omar, Maba, and Ahmadou Sheku is the lack of violence by an organized armed force. Cheikh Ahmadou Bamba actually abhorred violence.

Cheikh Ahmadou Bamba established his Mourride Brotherhood in 1886. His success rested on three factors. First, he incorporated his movement with the economic goals of the French. The major cash crop for the region is the peanut. Keeping in line with the concept that work is a form of worship, the Cheikh Ahmadou Bamba's talibes cultivated fields of peanuts all over present-day Senegal. Second, although he participated in an economy fostered by the French, he never totally allied himself with them and their program of assimilation. Thirdly and most importantly, he attracted the people in droves. Neither of the other two factors could be possible without the talibes.

This movement grew out of Cheikh Ahmadou Bamba's greater jihad, his personal striving to attain the highest level of devotion and religious scholarship. In 1887, Lat-Dior was defeated and killed in battle at Dhekkele. Albuuri Ndiaye was exiled from his kingdom of Jolof. The noble families and ceddo, all vassals of the kings, were displaced and/or disappointed. One good illustration of this is the case of Cheikh Ibra Fall.

The oral tradition, as reported by Serigne Bachirou Mbacké and *Le Journal Touba*, leaves us a story of Cheikh Ibra Fall when he united with Cheikh Ahmadou Bamba. Cheikh Ibra had received a divine inspiration in which he was told that a marabout by the name of Bamba would lead him and bring salvation to the masses. He had traveled to a town called Bamba and later to study with a marabout named Bamba Sylla. When he finally met Cheikh Ahmadou Bamba, he fell on his knees.[37] He then told Cheikh Ahmadou Bamba, "I left my house only to find such a guide. I only found his grave. The truth of my conviction to follow his example has caused me to achieve my objective. I vow to you not to gain anything of this world and to preoccupy myself with God and the future life."

The oral tradition leaves a record of Cheikh Ibra Fall as a devout man who was not like the majority of the nobles; his search, however, is parallel to the disillusioned nobles. Before the advent of Islam, the king received his authority and mysticism from the traditional religion. Being allied and related to the king, the nobles received the justification for their privelege and authority from the same base. When Islam came, certain marabout became vassals to the king directly or to the nobles. In exchange for protection and freedom to practice their religion, the marabout took on one of the roles of the traditional priests—that of court magician. The marabout made amulets and gris-gris in addition to saying special prayers for the particular nobles with whom they were aligned. Therefore, the nobles and kings did align their power with the new religion, although through the proverbial back door. The nobles and kings then used the sheer force of their power to protect said power against the renegade marabout in moments of jihad.

After the French took their power, the kings and the nobles (what was left of them) were disillusioned. They wanted a power structure relevant to them. In short there was a void. The illegitimate power of the French concentrated on regulating and protecting trade. Furthermore, the French operated within a metaphysical sphere that was too foreign to ever impose an authority that could affect a change in the hearts and minds of the masses. In other words, the French did not present a power structure capable of fulfilling the void left by the destroyed traditional governments.

The reasons for the charisma and staying power of Cheikh Ahmadou Bamba and his Mourride Brotherhood are many. Three reasons present themselves as the most compelling. First is what Cheikh Anta Diop termed the metaphysical reason. Cheikh Anta argues that in the traditional African mind, there is a separate spiritual world that mirrors our world and is very real and pertinent to the affairs and daily-life of humans. This is in contrast to the detached spiritual world of the modern euro-centric Christian view. Cheikh Anta sees this as a reason for the easy spread of Islam in sub-Saharan Africa. More pointedly, this is the reason for the appeal of Cheikh Ahmadou Bamba and his movement.

Another reason for the quick spread and perpetuation of Mouridisme is the nationalistic nature of Mourride theology. The Mourride Brotherhood was not the first mystic sect in the region. There was the Tidjani sect and the Khadre sect, but these sects originated in North Africa. The leaders of these sects also claimed a genealogical link to the prophet Mohammed. This is called sherifism. Cheikh Ahmadou Bamba had been an adherent to both of these sects at one time. When he found his independent mystic voice, however, he never succumbed to sherifism. This seemingly small fact is of great significance. In forgoing sherifism, Cheikh Ahmadou Bamba's theology turns the attention away from the leader and onto his devotion to his religion. The absence of sherifism also sends a message to the masses that one can reach the highest level of spirituality without claiming anything more than a spiritual link to the prophet Mohammed. Thus, his only affiliation with the Arab world was religious. He never even made the pilgrimage to Mecca or *hajj*. After his death, the Magale of Touba was established, which is an annual pilgrimage to the headquarters of Mouridism where Cheikh Ahmadou Bamba is entombed in the great mosque. This is not to say that he refused to take the hajj or discouraged it. On the contrary, he preached the tenets of Islam first and foremost. His life and troubles with the French made a *hajj* difficult at best and impossible at worst. All things considered, the local character of the Mourride tradition and theology supported a nationalistic base that underlined the jihad of Cheikh Ahmadou Bamba (as it had those who had come before) thereby providing an immediate relevance to the lives of the people, both noble and peasant.

The third reason for the attraction of Cheikh Ahmadou Bamba and his jihad was more immediately apparent to the people. The power of Cheikh Ahmadou Bamba attracted them. Not always because of a divine inspiration as in the case of Cheikh Ibra Fall, but because Cheikh Ahmadou Bamba possessed a power that the "infidel" French could not touch. His power was not upheld by the warfare in which the French had proven superior. Thus his power was not elusive. For the nobles and kings, Cheikh Ahmadou presented an alternative to submission or certain death by rebellion. This alternative also allowed the nobles and kings to keep their pride by not submitting to the toubab.

The second indigenous tariqa was the Layenne tariqa established by Mame Limamou Laye also known as Libasse Chaw. Unlike Sheikh Ahmadou Bamba, El Hajj Umar Tall, El Hajj Malik Sy, and all the other indigenous Islamic leaders, Mame Limamou was illiterate. He was also from a family of illiterate fishermen. His message and mission was geared especially for the Lebu people though others joined and still join the tariqa. The appeal of Mame Limamou's message is best understood in the light of Lebu culture.

Chapter 3

The Lebu

This chapter presents a brief history of the Lebu people, who live on the Peninsula of Cap-Vert in present-day Senegal. Cap-Vert, originally called Cabo-Verde (both names mean Green Cape) by the Portuguese, is the westernmost point of the African continent. The coordinates are 14° 44′ 41″ longitude and 17° 31′ 13″ latitude. It is a roughly triangular-shaped peninsula about 9 miles (15 kilometers) on each side. The rocky promontory point was produced by a combination of volcanic islands offshore and a land bridge that was the consequence of costal winds. The Lebu migrated to this area in waves over centuries.[1]

The area is arid with shrubs and a few trees like most of the rest of the Sahel. It rains three months of the year. The rains arrive in June and finish in early September. During the rest of the year, there is little to no rain. Intense agriculture is difficult under those conditions. The sea offers a bountiful source of food as well as facile transportation. The temperature remains constant most of the year with cold mornings during winter and slightly higher temperatures during the summer. The climate has placed limitations on economic opportunities. Trading and fishing have traditionally been the economic activities for this area.

The Lebu people have a long and complex history. Centuries of relative isolation created a situation where a small group of people developed a distinct culture and religion. The Lebu people are the result of mixing of people from other ethnic groups who all migrated to the coast bringing various gods and traditions. Most ethnic groups in the Senegambia region have lost most of their pre-Islamic religious practices. The Lebu, Serer, and Joola are the only ethnicities in the region who still have exclusive practitioners of the pre-Islamic religions. The Serer and the Joola resisted Islam until the later part of the 19th century. The Lebu, however, have had Muslims counted among them for centuries. How did the pre-Islamic religion survive? How much have the two religions borrowed from one another? Our goal in this chapter is to examine the culture, religion, and political organization of the Lebu and analyze how these features figure in Limamou Laye's mission. We must first pause to consider the sources and discuss how the colonial power structure through the new science of anthropology shaped a misunderstanding of African cultures, particularly the Lebu.

Review of Sources

Study of the Lebu began with French chroniclers and travelers. Passing descriptions of these people early on give today's historians and researchers only snippets of information. Toward the end of the 19th century as the French pursued their conquest in earnest, gaining an understanding of their new subjects became extremely important. Armed with the arrogance of conquerors and the assumption of white supremacy, specifically French supremacy, the early anthropologists left information smattered with their own shortcomings. G. T. Mollien mentioned the Lebu in his travel account on West Africa in 1818. G. J. Duchemin wrote an early account of the Lebu published in 1949. This work, while important to our study, is founded on ill-informed conjecture rather than systematic observation. Duchemin's work is relevant in that it takes into consideration the oral history record. Armand Pierre Angrande's 1951 work on the Lebu and their customs is noteworthy in that it gives them a Nilotic origin in Ancient Egypt. This idea seems to be connected to the oral account that the Lebu migrated from the east.

A much more detailed study was published in 1952. The authors, Balandier and Mercier, point out that their choice of the Lebu was influenced by the idiosyncrasies of the Lebu, that is, the geographical position of the Lebu on the peninsula Cap-Vert where their culture evolved into a unified identity specific to one little corner of the world. Armed with unity, the Lebu had had centuries of contact with Europeans, fought and won independence from the interior kingdom of Cayor, and established their own representative government all before the 19th century. Another outstanding feature of the Lebu was their economy's dependence on fishing. Citing the above mentioned facts, Balandier and Mercier's work is an important source of information but lacks an understanding of the interior logic of Lebu existence. The book descends into a listing of information taken from informers with suppositions serving as explanations. We understand that studying people as an outsider already carries so many difficulties. The added difficulty of the investigators obvious alliance with the colonizing power creates insurmountable limits. It is these limits that require supplemental voices to Balandier and Mercier's work.

The shortcomings of Balandier and Mercier's work are in many ways corrected once the Lebu people speak of themselves. Assane Sylla wrote *Le Peuple Lebou de la Presqu'ile du Cap-Vert* and published it in 1992. Lacking the intense details of Balandier and Mercier's book, Sylla's work gives insight into the reasoning of Lebu society. Sylla also transcribed and translated the account of traditional oral historian Mbaye Thiam (Cham). The strengths and weaknesses of these works lie in their authors who are both Lebu. The tendency toward self-congratulatory analysis is not totally avoided. The wealth of information, however, surpasses this weakness. In these works, the Lebu are no longer decreased to a mere subject of study. They become alive and human, stripped of their "otherness" that crippled previous studies.

The issues of how the Lebu are described in the sources correspond to the understanding of Limamou Laye's mission and the wider questions of Islam in Africa. A preoccupation with clarifying the differences in Africa and all things African is a major part of both public and academic discourse. Central to our concern is to demystify the African, particularly the Lebu, in order to legitimize these people as humans in pursuit of ideals and goals that all humans desire. Limamou Laye's expression of Islam stems from many issues surrounding him individually and the Lebu as a group, thus opening the discussion to the seemingly obvious observation of his and his people's humanity and is intended to cast away the ignominious specter of anthropological subjects thereby exposing an understanding of how Laye's activities are possible first as a human and secondly as a Lebu and then a Muslim.

Origins of the Lebu

The Lebu people are found on the coast of present-day Senegal at the peninsula called Cap-Vert. By tradition the Lebu were thought to have migrated there from East Africa by way of North Africa, through present-day Mauritania to the Jolof Empire. However, the claim of East African origin belongs to myth than to historical reality (though it is not beyond historical possibility). The above-mentioned assertion that the Lebu came from Ancient Egypt echoes many such ethnopolitical claims that arose as an answer to the assertion of white supremacy during the days of colonization. The Lebu obviously migrated from somewhere east of where they are now because migration from West of where they are would require maritime travel. Maritime travel is not beyond the possibility of any people, but the Lebu oral record displays an orientation towards the east, the direction from where they started their original movement.

According to the oral record, the Lebu continued migrating to the Kingdom of Cayor and eventually to the coast. The migration was gradual as they came in small groups of various ethnic origins. The oral record cites the reason for the constant move of the Lebu, as their refusal to be dominated politically or culturally. Some suspect that the word Lebu means defiant warrior based on the Wolof word *lubu,* which means bellicose warrior. Balandier and Mercier offer other etymological possibilities though all are inconclusive.[2]

According to oral tradition, while in Jolof, the Lebu along with two other groups rebelled against King Birame Coumba Jemme. Once the insurgents were defeated, the Lebu fled to the farthest provinces of the empire. Another version reports that during the reign of Amari Ngone Mbengue, his maternal nephew Jaja (whose father was the king of Trarza) orchestrated a *coup d'état* supported by a portion of the Trarza armed forces. After usurping his uncle's throne, Jaja became the founding emperor of the Jolof Empire taking the throne name Njaajaan Njiye.[3]

Amari Ngone Mbengue, his family, and loyal followers left the Jolof Empire. Before leaving his kingdom, Amari consulted the spirits or *tuur* who in turn told him to go to the southwest where happiness and prosperity awaited him. All this happened in the 16th century. The

Lebu migration reportedly began in the 15th century and continued gradually.[4] One could say it continued into the colonial period because the Lebu always had a good reputation for taking in refugees and fugitives without asking questions. According to tradition, the Lebu made the promise to always take in and protect fugitives and refugees as an act of thanksgiving to the *tuur* who promised them the land.[5]

The Lebu arriving gradually found the Sosse people living on the peninsula. As the Lebu gradually became more numerous, in the second half of the 15th century they fought and defeated the Sosse people, killing their king around 1470. Having secured the land, the Lebu populace continued to grow and began to establish villages. They developed a political organization that evolved into a confederation of quasi-republics headed by the Serigne Ndakaru.[6]

The oral tradition cites the settlement experience of one family as a probable pattern. Ma Fall N'Doye was one of the founders of the first village known as Mberoum Thialam. His wife was from Jolof, and they had three sons and one daughter, who are said to be the ancestors of most of the Lebu. Ndoye's grandson, Birame Yacine N'Doye founded the village of M'Bidjeum. Other N'Doye descendants established Chaden, Danki-Mali and many other villages. Amary Ngone Mbengue established the village of Mbukhekhe. This pattern continued with different ones founding villages and people from earlier villages moving there along with new Lebu emigrants from Cayor.[7] There is some speculation as to the proper ethnicity of the Lebu. Although they speak Wolof, their names are traditionally Serer names.[8] This fact supports the assertion that the Lebu were of mixed origins.

In 1549, the Jolof Empire, which was really a confederation of smaller kingdoms, fell apart. The kingdoms of Waalo, Cayor, Bawol, and Saloum all became independent of the kingdom of Jolof. The Dameel (the title of the ruler of Cayor) of Cayor claimed the peninsula of Cap-Vert as part of Cayor. The Lebu paid annual tribute to the Dameel. The Lebu, however, were involved in a lucrative trade with the French on the island of Goree that the French rented from the Lebu. Once the Dameel discovered the amount of guns, and other goods the Lebu received from the European trade, he demanded that the Lebu pay him part of it and sent an *alkati* or customs official to collect his share.

The Lebu continuously refused to pay their taxes to Cayor. The Dameel in turn sent punitive military expeditions to the Lebu. The Lebu resisted and, in the process, organized their defense and developed an effective military. During the reign of Latsukaabé Ngoné Dièye (1697-1719), the Dameel's forces were driven back. It was not until 1798[9], however, during the reign of the Dameel Amary Ngoné Della Coumba that the Lebu defeated Cayor and established the Lebu confederated "republic." The Lebu built walls for protection against raids from Cayor because the Dameel did not recognize Lebu independence until approximately 15 years later when Jaal Joop's son Moctar was Serigne NDakaru, or the ruler of Dakar and the confederation of Lebu villages. Cayor recognized Lebu independence and established good relations with the new state.[10]

Political Organization

Prior to their victory over the Dameel in 1798, the Lebu villages had only united in matters of defense with a very loose political structure headed by the *jaraf* who operated as a head of state. The *ndeye ji rew* served as a minister of the interior and foreign affairs acting both as ambassador and mediator in inter-Lebu disputes. The *saltigué* was the minister of defense responsible for organizing the armed forces in time of war. The *saltigué* was also responsible for the well-being of the whole Lebu community. In that role, he was responsible for the natural resources as well as keeping good relations with the *tuur* so that no harm came to the community. Each village had a *lamane*, or village chief, whose primary job was to regulate the land ownership in the village. There was a confederate-wide *lamane* with the title *mafane*, who essentially handled land ownership issues concerning the whole confederacy.

These officers were aided by a bi-cameral assembly. The upper house was the *jambour* or assembly of old wise men composed of 36 men all over the age of 50 comprised of three representatives chosen from each of the 12 quarters of Dakar. The Jambour was a legislative assembly that decided on all important decisions before they were taken. The lower house was the *frey* or the assembly of young elected men consisting of forty-eight men comprised of four chosen from each of the twelve quarters of Dakar. The Frey, presided over by the Ndeye ji frey, was responsible for enforcing the decisions made by the Jambour through voting. The Jambour, presided over by the Ndèye ji Jambour, also elected the Jaraf, the Saltigué, and the Ndèye ji rew from certain families delegated to each position. The position of Jaraf was reserved for men who could matrilineally trace their origins to the Soumbediounes, which was comprised of the following clans: Khonkh-bopp, Wanère, and Jassirato.

After the victory in 1798, the Lebu decided to create a more centralized state. Jaal Joop, a marabout who fled the dameel after an unsuccessful jihad, came to the Lebu where his maternal clan, the Mbengue lived. Because of his status as an intellectual, his connection with one of the oldest families in the area, and his active participation in the victorious battle, he was unanimously elected to a new position called *serigne ndakarou.* The small but strong Islamic community among the Lebu wanted to see one of their own at the head of the state. Originally the position was not political but religious as *serigne* is a traditional title for marabouts, but Jaal Joop immediately took on roles of head of state. The mandate of the Jaraf was demoted to minister of finance and agriculture. The Saltigue kept his job as defense minister, but the religious role was given to a newly created officer, Imam Ratib (or Imam of the cult of rab). The responsibility for the fishing industry on which the Lebu economy depended went to a new official the Barquthie. The Khali was the minister of justice. These ministers along with the Ndeye ji frey were all appointed by the Serigne Ndakarou in consultation with the Ndeye ji Rew and the Ndeye Jambour all of whom were elected by the Jambour. There was also a privy council chosen from the most respected members of the Jambour whose job was strictly consultative.[11]

Lebu Traditional Religion

As mentioned above, the Lebu are not originally of the Wolof people, but they have accepted and adopted Wolof culture and language after settling on the peninsula of present-day Dakar, Senegal. They migrated to that area from the northwest area of present day Senegal in the 16th century.[12] Their main economic activities were fishing and agriculture, with animal husbandry as a complementary occupation.

The Lebu religion involves the worship of ancestor spirits and what the Islamized Lebu call jinn (genies) or spirits. The Wolof names are *tuur* and *rab*. Some sources site the *tuur* as ancestral spirits and the *rab* as ancient descendants who have ascended to a god like status.[13] Other sources site the rab as genies with no connection to humans.[14] The Lebu sometimes use one or the other term to refer to spirits in general. Whatever the case, these spirits are a prominent part of the religion and are deeply integrated into the Lebu identity. The Lebu people secured their safety and good health through their service to the *tuur* and *rab*. The tuur and rab are appeased with gifts of food, ceremonies, and small sacrifices. When things go wrong, the spirits are consulted in order to make things right.[15]

The tuur are said to live close to humans and usually come in the form of animals. The *rab* are more distant and powerful. Each house of an adherent to the traditional religion had a *xamb*, which is an altar dedicated to the family tuur and rab. These structures cannot be removed or damaged without express permission from the spirits that they honor with proper ceremony. It is at the *xamb* that the adherents sacrifice animals to the *tuur* while inquiring and/or appeasing the spirit for some infraction that caused sickness or misfortune. Sacrifices are also made regularly in order to keep good relations with the spirits.[16]

Mondays and Thursdays are cult days where the spirits are offered milk, millet, and kola nuts. The *ndopkat* are agents of the cult. *Boroom tuur*, literally masters of the tuur, are priests, usually females, who act as intermediaries between humans and the spirits. The *boroom tuur* are attached through their families to a particular rab/tuur and in their role as intermediaries, they officiate at all ceremonies honoring their particular spirits. The *boroom tuur* are consulted on every stage of an adherent's life and are paid huge fees when they conduct healing ceremonies. Once a year big ceremonies are held for the big tuur of each city.[17]

When the Lebu migrated to Cap-Vert they were directed to come by the tuur. Once there, they made a pact with the tuur to serve them in return for protection and prosperity. Each family is devoted to at least one tuur/rab in addition to the ancestral spirits. The rules providing for the sanctity of the xamb are followed as closely as those for the rules of Islam. The central idea of the traditional religion is one of appeasing the rab/tuur. When anything goes wrong in life, it is the result of some offense in the spirit world. Thus, one has to identify which one of the tuur/rab is offended so that he/she can be properly appeased. The ndopkat are the only people who can communicate directly with the tuur/rab. Once consulted, the ndopkat are compensated for their service. If a ceremony must be performed, the ndopkat is again compensated. In such a troublesome world, the role of ndeopkat can be lucrative, though none of them would ever admit to it.[18]

The rab and tuur have genealogies. Some are said to have accompanied the Lebu to the coast while others are said to have already been there, particularly the water spirits. There are accounts of spirits coming and then going back to Cayor. One came and had a daughter then left her daughter. Some marry other spirits. In short, their world parallels the human world. The rab are said to live in trees, rocks, or water. These spirits cause good and harm, thus the necessity for appeasement. Some of the rab are said to have converted to Islam. Muslims often have ceremonies called *samp* for the converted rab.[19]

Each of the Lebu villages has a spirit who is thought to be the protector of that village. These protector spirits are honored annually for their protection and throughout the year offerings are left on their altars. One informant told me that whenever a new religious idea is introduced to an area the protector spirit comes to check out the new idea in order to make sure his/her interests are not negatively affected. This informant reported having seen Mame Coumba Sene attend a meeting where his marabout was proseletyzing. The marabout recognized her and pointed her out to him as she exited the meeting. As protector spirits, the economic and spiritual well-being of the community is their responsibilities. This does not include other spiritual problems of individuals. Those problems are handled by that individual and his/her priest/priestess.

The Lebu practice most commonly known to outsiders is the ndeupe ceremony. This is a healing ritual, which involves sacrifice, dance, and spirit possession. First the sickness is diagnosed, which whatever the case, is only a consequence of a spiritual problem. There are four possible problems, sorcery, maraboutic magic, possession by a jinn/ demon, or possession by an ancestral spirit. Once the problem is discerned, the patient is taken into the house of the priestess where an animal is sacrificed. The patient is then bathed in the blood of the animal. Next there is another ritual where griots come and sing to evoke the spirits. The spirits then come and possess the patient and the dancers and sometimes others in attendance. Later the patient goes into a trance and dances while in possession of the spirit(s).[20]

Though there are men ndeopkat, most ndeopkat are women. The Lebu are thoroughly Islamized today. However, the traditional practices continue usually presided over by women. In the traditional religion one is either initiated or uninitiated. The initiates come to be so through a possession that can only be cured through an ndeupe. Once the person is cured he/she becomes an initiate. The initiate undergoes a period of study that can last for decades, during which he/she learns the secrets of the cult of rab and the healing practices. Thus, one does not choose to become an initiate, one of the tuur/rab chooses an individual.

Lebu religion has a focus on the righting of any wrong. Like many other African religions, the religion of the Lebu operates from the assumption that everything in the physical realm has a spiritual antecedent. If balance exists in the spiritual and physical world, one can live in peace. All rituals and practices are geared toward keeping the balance. When there is some infraction either by a human or a malevolent spirit, ceremonies and rites are required to bring things back into balance. Problems in the physical world are always the manifestation of some imbalance in the spiritual realm. Thus the rituals to bring healing are always aiming at affecting change in the spiritual world.

This concentration on the unseen is indicative of the Lebu worldview which consists of an overarching concept that the spirit world is the greater reality. This type of thinking gives the adherent a greater appreciation for the mundane things in life. As everything one experiences with his/her five senses is just a manifestation of a greater reality hidden from the natural eye, everything is importantly symbolic. In our further discussion of Layennes, we will see that Limamou Laye's clothing, speech, and even the timing of his announcement are all manifestations of a greater reality.

Islam among the Lebu

The caravans from Mauritania saw the area around present-day Dakar as the end of the line for them, which placed the Lebu at the crossroads of two trade lines. Sometime during the 16th century, the Lebu began to convert to Islam through the efforts of the Muslim caravans. Their Islam was a syncretic religion combined with the traditional religious practices indigenous to the area. There is no indication that the implantation of Islam in the 16th century was superficial as Balandier and Mercier contend. Another wave of Islamization came to the Lebu by way of refugees from the jihad of 1795 in the Wolof kingdom of Cayor to the northwest of the Lebu.[21]

Marabout fleeing the wrath of the dameel (king) of Cayor in late 18th century ran southwest and found refuge among the Lebu. The Maraboutic family that established their suzerainty over the Lebu is the Joop family. Jaal Joop was the first of these leaders. The Joop family settled among the Lebu and established an Islamic theocracy after having led the Lebu in a successful rebellion against the Kingdom of Cayor. There has been dispute over whether the Joop established a republic or a kingdom.[22] There definitely were traces of both forms of government present in the Lebu political organization, but assigning a foreign label to the government is irrelevant to real observation. In particular it goes beyond the scope and purpose of this study. Thus it is sufficient for us to say that the Lebu had a well-organized government that defies an appropriate Western label.

Popular Islam developed in these areas as a result of a combination of rituals from traditional religion and orthodox Islam along with an oral tradition developed from this interchange. The Joop family is a family steeped in Islamic scholarship and of great spiritual stature. But they settled down among the Lebu and took wives from the local population. This had an indelible effect on their Islam. The Lebu women were usually the guardians of the traditional religion. With such hands rocking their cradles, the Joop family's Islam adapted to

Lebu traditions. Although the Lebu were mostly Muslim by the 17th century, a significant portion of the population practiced the native religion exclusively, while others practiced the native rituals alongside Islam.[23]

Lebu Islam

The Lebu hold on to their traditional spiritual practices and are devout Muslims. The major question is how do the Lebu reconcile the dictum of Islam with their pre-Islamic practices? Central to this arrangement is the agreement on the divine. Lebu acknowledge that there is no God but God and Muhammad is his prophet. The rab/tuur, however are not gods, but spirits. The Lebu ancestors learned of the rab/tuur and made pacts with them that cannot be denied. The Lebu in turn honor the rab/tuur with annual feast days and regular offering, in return, the rab/tuur are consulted in times of crises and hold up their end of the pact by helping the Lebu.

Another major part of the peaceful coexistence of the two religions is the integration of Islam into the traditional religious practices. When offerings are made at the xamb, the Lebu bless the occasion with the Islamic incantation *bissmeelah ah rahmani raheem* . . . In doing so they offer praises to God and purify the act. On the grand feast days of the tuur of the various Lebu cities, the same Islamic blessing is uttered when preparing the animal sacrifices. During the ndeupe ceremony, Muslim prayers are also often used along with the traditional incantations. The ndeupe and other rituals and ceremonies are scheduled so they do not conflict with Islamic prayer times and/or festivals.

The integration of practice does not cause any theological misgivings in the mind of the Lebu. The rab/tuur are anthropomorphic. As such when the Lebu converted, the rab/tuur also converted. Since the rab/tuur are part of the umma they must be celebrated in Islamic fashion. Like venerated family members however, the rab/tuur are deserving of honor and respect and they merit the festivals and sacrifices. The rab/tuur are all called *mame* which in the Wolof language means grandmother/grandfather. Thus in the same manner that one honors a departed grandparent with a Quran reading and festival, they fete the rab/tuur. Granted there are many Lebu who do not participate regularly in the traditional religious activities, even among them there are those who consult the ndokpat when they are ill or when misfortune befalls.

As mentioned in the previous chapter, scholars have always analyzed this type of Islam as "not quite Islam." From the very beginning of French intellectual inspection of Islam, they made a distinction between Islam and *Islam noir*, which is somehow not as good as Islam. Lebu Islam would fall firmly into the French explanation of *Islam noir*. Our basic assumption in analyzing Lebu Islam is that there is no monolithic Islam. The portability of the religion requires cultural adaptability. Otherwise converting to Islam would amount to cultural suicide.

In the context of the Lebu community, their culture and identity are intertwined. As they are not an ethnicity composed of people from various ethnic origins, the Lebu culture is formulated from various groups with a Wolof ethnic base and a Wolof dialect for communication. For a Lebu to disengage from his/her culture is essentially for him to stop being a Lebu. Thus the Lebu, like countless other peoples, had to negotiate an agreement with Islam. The Islamic teaching on *jiin* is really crucial to the negotiation.[24] The rab/tuur became jiin and Islamized and Lebu Muslims did not lose their identity.[25] Lebu Islam, however, is not Lebuized Islam. Lebu Islam is just the imposition of Islam on a Lebu superstructure. Limamou Laye Lebuized Islam through another process discussed in Chapter 4.

Colonization

In 1857, while the Lebu were celebrating the end of Ramadan, the French paid them a visit. Thinking their friends and tenants (the French were renting Goree from the Lebu) had come to participate in their celebration, the Lebu were delighted. The French were not paying a social call but a business call to inform the Lebu that there would be no more rent payments coming. The French went on to say that they were not only proclaiming their suzerainty over Goree, but also the Lebu themselves. After centuries of dealing with European, the Lebu had now to readjust their thinking to fit this new relationship.

For the most part, life among the Lebu continued as before. The Lebu governmental structure was left in place. Gradually taxes were assessed and collected, landscape changed as infrastructure was constructed, and the lives of the Lebu were changed forever. As these changes were gradual, it is difficult to ascertain the level of crisis that these changes elicited in Lebu society. Assane Sylla states that the French never executed any violent act against the Lebu.[26] The French allowed them to retain their system of government with the French governor having the final say on major decisions. In other words, the French ruled with the system already in place.

As Dakar developed into an urban area and eventually the capitol of French West Africa (Afrique occidentale francaise or AOF) and later capitol of the Republic of Senegal, the Lebu found themselves in possession of prime real estate. The French had their eye on Lebu land. They had already appropriated much through negotiations with the Lebu rulers even before they conquered the Lebu. The archives document instances of unrest among the Lebu particularly during the yellow fever epidemic of 1914.

The Lebu, were initially hostile to French colonization, prohibiting their children from going to the Catholic run French schools. As things changed, the government in Dakar effectively negotiated a space for the Lebu in colonial Dakar. As part of the *Quatre Communes* (Dakar, Rufisque, Goree, and St. Louis), the Lebu were given French citizenship and the franchise. Their voting privileges enabled them to elect first Blaise Diagne (who was Lebu through his mother's mother). The Lebu later used their vote as a leverage to improve their situation. Early on the Lebu had allied themselves with the French Métis of Goree which led to a lucrative exchange. Many Lebu women had become concubines of Frenchmen and gave birth to the Métis community of Goree. With the consolidation of colonization, the Lebu possession of the franchise empowered them. Thus the Lebu experience with colonization, though not totally smooth, was comparatively easy. Many of them have reaped substantial financial benefits.

The historical consistency of government, culture, language, and religion of Lebu is a unique situation in post-independence Senegal. In a society where most other ethnicities have become or are becoming thoroughly "wolofized" the Lebu retain their cultural institution and their particular dialect of Wolof. This strength of ethnic identity transformed Islamic interpretation from something foreign into a home grown religion. French suzerainty became just another instance in history. Modern roads, hospitals, buildings, and schools did not encroach on Lebu identity. On the contrary Lebu identity exhibited an elasticity that enabled the Lebu to adapt to their changing surroundings.

Lebu elasticity is no where better exhibited than in the Lebu's attitude towards Islam. Lebu Islam has come to dominate the community. This spiritual environment gave birth to and nurtured Limamou Laye providing the building materials for the Layenne tariqa.

Lebu Identity, Black Nationalism, and French Colonization

When one speaks of the development of an identity it must not be precluded that those who are constructing the identity start from scratch. Identity evolves naturally from a people's physical environment, positioning in or around an existing society, as well as their political reality which exists in correlation to their social positioning. Thus we can easily deduce that in order for an identity to be formulated, there must be at least the above mentioned conditions, but just as physical evolution is infinite so is sociocultural evolution. Keeping this in mind it is imperative that we recognize certain variables that play a significant role in the continually, though gradually, changing conditions pertinent to identity construction. First, are the changes in nature which often threaten the security and even the existence of the people. Second are the technological innovations which inevitably lead to social innovations. Thirdly and most important to our discussion are the rise and fall in governments as well as the informal (for lack of a better word) power structures that often lie outside the real scope of government intervention. The third variable is usually the result of the first and second or both. Colonization is an example of this type of variable.

It is impossible to discuss or even conceptualize identity formation in the world outside of Europe without recognizing the predominate role of European colonization in this world. Edward Said put forward a useful model of the "Orient" being a creation of "Occidents" based on certain realities of the East yet predicated by the power/servant relationship between the West and East and rooted in the uncontestable assumption of Western superiority.[27] Unlike many scholars, Said did not make the identity of the people of the East centered on "Orientalism." On the contrary, he acknowledges that Orientalism ignores the humanity of these peoples and reduces them to mere objects in a construction of the "Orient." The application of Said's model to European concepts of Africans is essential to us in our posture as "occidents" trying to understand Lebu identity. In doing so, we are confronted with the creation of an African identity in response to the identity that Europeans created for Africans. Colonized Africans developed an identity of inferiority vis-à-vis Europe and America which inhibits African political, social, and economic evolution.

Before we continue our discussion we must appraise the prevailing realities of our language and its role in the Euro-centric power play that pervades academics as well as world politics. Europeans created Africa just as the Occident created the Orient. Prior to Europeans informing them, the Congo, Nguni, Berber, and Mande peoples did not know that they were Africans. Western explorers and missionaries came to inform the native peoples that they were backward and that there was a better way of life. As European conquest of the world's second largest continent progressed with Europeans playing one African state against another, the realization of Black Consciousness began to grip the minds of the peoples. In other words the Congo, Nguni, Berber, and Mande as well as all others became Africans because Europeans demonstrated that their otherness trumped all other considerations and previous relationships. As most precolonial African states were the victims of severe localization in thought and deed, their introduction to World politics and economy was through a subservient position as the colonized. Thus, the seeds of European exploration and colonization produced Africa.

When we use the term Colonized Africans it refers to people who have, because of their exposure to French education, accepted French Civilization and its superiority to their native civilization. This includes the citoyens of the four communes of Dakar and the evolués throughout the AOF as well as the subsequent generations of schoolchildren. For the sake of understanding identity it is necessary to distinguish between the Colonized African and the other segments of the population who had no choice but to accept French military superiority but could never fathom European cultural superiority, much less accept it. The Colonized Africans as the policy makers in present day Africa are the focus of our discussion. This is not to say that European colonization did not affect the identities of those in the second group, as the political reality changed when the French took over the area; but their distance from the seat of political power afforded them much freedom from French interference in their everyday lives and thus the evolution of their identity.

The Colonized Africans did not have such freedom. From the outset of French Colonization of the AOF, they impressed upon the indigenous population an identity born from centuries of speculation which, when faced with real Africans, simply co-opted certain facts in order to support the prevailing ideological conceptualization of 'Africaness'. In his edited work *Race and the Enlightenment,* Emmanuel Eze compiles some of these attitudes which predate French colonization by 200 years. The Europeans had just rediscovered Greek "knowledge" with the help of the Arabs, who would in turn become victims of this "knowledge." Eze's work assembled excerpts from some of Europe's most celebrated authors in which the only consensus in the disparate group is that Europeans are superior to the rest of the world. Johann Gottfried von Herder offers the most liberal approach to race but his insistence on explaining the Black color can easily be interpreted as buying into the racist ideologies of his age. As the white skin is the "ideal" the variation has to be explained in order to establish their humanity. More unquestionably racist remarks set the tone for the work, and no other part of the work clearly exhibits the attitude than the quote from Kant's "On National Characteristics" where he cites a story of Father Labat who tells of an African carpenter who after the priest admonished him for severity toward his wives answered that Whites are strange in that they give their wives so much freedom but later complain when the wives cause trouble. Kant says maybe there's something of merit in the quote but concludes that: "in short, this fellow was quite black from head to foot, a clear proof that what he said was stupid.[28]

The most powerful aspect of Eze's work is that it displays a systematic ideological construct supported by a pseudo-scientific approach to examining the world and in turns supports the white supremacy ideology which later becomes the underlying principle of French Colonial Policy and all European Colonial Policy for that matter. The writers in Eze's work, however did not create the idea of the inferiority of the other, this began with the Greeks and Romans as Eze states. William Cohen more specifically discusses the ancient Greeks' and Romans' attitudes towards Africa when he explains that "the ancients' climatic theory also emphasized that extreme temperature made people act in extreme savage ways . . ."[29] Cohen's work also examines another aspect of the early European literature on Africans in that it looks at the work of travelers on which the writers of Eze's work based their writings. Just as with the Enlightenment writers who were preoccupied with the causation of the Africans' pigmentation, so were the travelers and missionaries who wrote in the 15th through the 18th centuries. Led by Leo Africanus, these travelers also equated Africa and it's inhabitants with all the negative characteristics of human kind.[30] From these early examples, the would-be French colonizers constructed an identity for Africans that would serve them throughout colonization.

What was this French created image of Africans? We have already examined the precolonial notions of Blacks. We have not pointed out, however, that these notions were mitigated by slavery. Individual Frenchmen did not have total tunnel vision when Blacks were concerned. As Cohen has so eloquently pointed out, the French acted one way in dealing with Blacks as slave masters and with Blacks as rulers and customers/producers.[31] But when French official policy is examined, we see the overriding principle of white supremacy played out in laws prohibiting Blacks from entering France, and the treatment of Blacks after the abolition of slavery. The slaves of Imperial France lived in the New World. Once these slaves were freed, they were eventually made into citizens. Before the *mission civilatrice* had been articulated, it was played out in the Antillean colonies. After undergoing proper initiation and education into the French system, Antillean Blacks were used to govern the African empire. Furthermore, France granted citizenship and the same rights to Africans living in the four Communes of present day Senegal. Thus they began the same process of civilization with African Blacks. The prevailing notion was that Blacks had no culture or civilization worthy of note and that the only way up for them was through assimilation to French culture. Furthermore, it was the duty of France as a civilized nation to help the poor savage Blacks to attain civilization. Thus schoolchildren in the Antilles and the four communes of Dakar begin reciting in the late 19th century about their "ancestors" the Gauls. This absurdity was lost on the French architects of colonization because they saw the Gauls as the cultural ancestors of these poor African schoolchildren. Eventually, some in the colonial service began to see the possibility of the Africans evolving themselves under the tutelage of the French, but even with this more liberal view, the idea of the supremacy of French civilization and government undermined any real effort at allowing the Africans cultural independence.

Now that we have clearly examined the idea of Blacks in the AOF, we must look at the Colonized Blacks response to the conditions. At this point our analysis becomes a bit more difficult. We do not have these people around to interview, so we must look at the way French civilization was played out in their lives along with some examples from this group. Memmi's work on the colonized does not apply to all of the AOF. None of the colonies in the AOF were settler colonies, thus the conditions under which the Algerians lived about which Memmi writes are not totally applicable. The Colonized Africans of the AOF had an existence similar to the colonized of Algeria. The Colonized African of the AOF underwent French education, in some cases extensive French education that usually ended in France. This education was more than just fundamental knowledge, it was designed to teach the student how to be a good educated Frenchman.

Memmi speaks of two choices that the colonized make: either to try to ameliorate their situation by making themselves like the colonizer, or opposing colonization. Our Colonized African has clearly made the first choice. "The colonized does not seek merely to enrich himself with the colonizer's virtues. In the name of what he hopes to become, he sets his mind on impoverishing himself, tearing himself away from his true self."[32] The result of this self-hatred is a self perpetuating internalized oppression, which plays out in a suppression of everything that is similar to the Colonized African's past. There are varying degrees of this response. Memmi cites an interracial marriage as the most extreme.[33]

In the case of the AOF where there were mostly Muslims and Animists natives, the Muslims usually kept their religion where as the Animists usually converted at least nominally to Chrisitianity. As Christopher Harrison and David Robinson both illustrate, France eventually came to an uneasy truce with Islam in its African possession, thus it became alright to be a Muslim.[34] Animists never enjoyed such latitude, thus they usually saw conversion as a step forward. In the eyes of the French colonial government, the Christians were natural allies as opposed to the Muslims. The sheer numbers of Muslims forced the authorities to develop a workable relationship with them. There were many interracial sexual relationships however, in the early stages of colonization between colonial officials and African concubines which continued until the end of the French colonial era, and also between African students who studied in France and the French.. The Africans usually married the white women and raised their children as Frenchmen, whereas the Frenchmen usually took their concubines as a convenience and at best they recognized the children and educated them. The religious example and sexual relationships both display the unevenness of the colonial/native relationship and the pathology of the Colonized Africans.

After the education conducted under the civilizing mission, and in some cases marital relationship with the oppressor, the Colonized African is no longer a member of his ethnic group or of his French prescribed group of Africans as he does not fit the description of the indolent, ignorant savage. What then does he do, he is forced to construct a new identity. Alioune Diop stated it best.

"Incapable of entirely returning to our original traditions or of assimilating to Europe, we had the feeling we were forming a new race, mentally mixed, but which was not aware of its originality and had not become self-conscious. Uprooted? We were precisely to the degree that we had not yet defined our position in the world and we were stranded between two societies, without recognizing meaning in either one, foreigners to both."[35]

Out of this type of confusion, we see the profoundly disgruntled Negritude movement led by two icons of French literature, Aime Cesaire and Leopold Senghor. Senghor later went on to be the first president of Senegal for over twenty years and the first person of African descent to be elected to the *Academie Francaise.* He married a French woman who became the "first lady" of Senegal. Of the same generation was Houphouet Boigny who became the first president of the Ivory Coast and as such he granted citizenship to Frenchmen and invited French technicians and other trained workers to come and build his country only to the detriment of the intellectual and technical development of the Ivorian populace. These men's lives are indicative of the confusion that Alioune Diop describes in the quote above. The identities that they created are parallel to the nations that they created. These nations are dependent on France for everything and have not evolved into the self-sufficient productive nations that they could be. The condition of being caught between two societies, two modes of existence forged a depressed identity that depended on France for a level of unattainable civilization and stood on native civilization as a shame that could not be hidden or totally disguised. Just like the Holocaust survivors and the freedmen of the American South, the Colonized Africans bequeathed their confounded identity to their natural and political offspring who in some cases perpetuated their weaknesses and succeed in creating a continent full of woes.

In his work "*God Alone is King": Islam and Emancipation in Senegal,* James Searing takes exception to the historian's tendency to portray colonization as the defining moment in African history. He insists that colonization can be properly understood if it is looked at as another event in a chain of events that each have cause/effect relationships. Searing's assessment is accurate, but one cannot ignore the profound changes that European colonization wrought in Africa. The French definitively altered the political reality in West Africa which became the AOF, and thusly created a situation for many natives to choose either to accept colonization or to flee to the hinterland and fight or hide amongst the populace whose lives were not greatly affected by colonization. Those who accepted saw that their only means for surviving in the new environment was to assimilate as much as possible.

They submitted to French education. They wore French clothing in spite of its impracticality in a tropical climate. In some cases they married French spouses and accepted the French religion. The French with their *mission civilatrice* offered them the chance to be Black Frenchmen, and these Colonized Frenchmen followed all the rules and steps established for their attainment of Frenchness. But in the end they were deceived because they neglected to recognize the impregnable fortress of white supremacy made French civilization unattainable for Blacks. The fact that colonization is based on white supremacy was always omitted from their lessons. They learned the code language of the French racist without the ability to decipher the code. Thus in the end they were disappointed but not enough to abandon their Frenchness. On the contrary, after colonization they bemoan their Africanness and make their lives in France or they return to the mother country and continue the *mission civilatrice* with earnest. As people who strove to better their environment by whatever means, could these men be considered nationalists?

Nationalism is an idea that the distinctiveness of a group of people requires that they create a political entity in order to survive. For the nationalist, the entire world is seen through the prism of his/her nationalist agenda. All things outside the interior mundane things of the group are seen as how they will affect the group. The individuals see the group as a larger more important individual. Nationalism requires myths that bind, symbols, and a common ethos that gives shape and definition to the people vis-à-vis others who are not members of the group. Many ethnic nationalist groups are based on the myth of a common ancestor or a shared historical experience that shaped the group's destiny.

Lebu identity was well developed before the French came to Senegal. A major part of their identity was their resistance to others who wanted to subjugate them. Lebu group identity is not based on a unifying ancestor or group experience. The Lebu are a grouping of people who migrated to the coast from other parts of the region. Their location along with a fierce determination to govern themselves are the factors that unified them along with their concentration on fishing as a trade. Though there was a core of Lebu who initially migrated to the Cap Vert, many others migrated later and were included. The Lebu tradition of accepting those who were running from the authorities did not endear them to the authorities in Cayor, but it helped to enlarge their numbers and contributed to the forging of an identity that did not resort to the exclusivity found in most ethnic groups.

The position of the Lebu at the apex of an extensive trading network made exclusivity inconducive to their survival. They traded with the Europeans as well as with the Arabs with ease. However, their group cohesiveness cannot be responsibly overlooked. Much of it came from their particular history as a group in search of freedom from the monarchal traditions as well as their occupation as master fishermen. The oral tradition holds that the Lebu were fishermen on the upper Senegal before their exodus to the coast. They are said to have learned the secret rituals of fishing from the *Tiebalo,* the fishing caste of the Peulh ethnic group. The Tiebalo are considered to be the only group who are better fishermen than the Lebu. The oral tradition states that in teaching the Lebu to fish, the Tiebalo kept some of the mystical secrets to themselves.

Other tradition cite a mystic origin of certain Lebu families from mer-people and or water spirits. The Njie family is said to be descended from Njanjan Njie who was a water spirit. In Senegal most people acknowledge that there is a mystical connection between the Lebu and the creatures of the sea. Even in the 21st centuries, one of my informants who is a non-Lebu fisherman who proudly proclaims to know his trade well admits to the superiority of the Lebu in the fishing industry. In most rural agricultural societies, everyone is a farmer who does something else between the growing seasons. The Lebu are fishermen who farm on the side.

The Lebu position as a weaker people fleeing from stronger better organized kingdoms required an interdependence, which also was a factor that bound them together. During their war with the Damel cited above, as well as with all of their other wars, they were forced to work together in order to organize defense which is the first step of what led to them making the leap from a grouping of independent villages to a coherent political organization. Lebu nationalism growing from a common occupation and social situation has given them a particular condition that fostered a common outlook in spite of ethnic differences. This common outlook colored all individual Lebus including Limamou Laye who proclaimed his mission to the world, but to the Lebu first.

Chapter 4

The Early Life of Libasse Chaw (Thiaw)

This chapter will present the narrative of Limamou Laye's life before he proclaimed his mission. Based on the account given by his hagiographer Sheikh Muktar Lô, this chapter will also analyze the content of the hagiography. We will examine the life of a typical young man in mid-19th century Lebu community in an attempt to understand the experiences that shaped Limamou Laye's worldview and thereby his mission.

In discussing our subject we will employ the name Libasse Chaw and Limamou Laye. They are one and the same person; however, there is a duality of the existence symbolized by the two names. Libasse Chaw is the historical personage of the colonial record. Limamou Laye is also in the colonial record but only as the founder and leader of the Layenne tariqa. Libasse Chaw is the boy who became Limamou Laye. The name Limamou is the Wolofised version of the Arabic Al-Imam. Laye is the diminutive of the Wolof Yallah meaning Allah. Limamou Laye is thus al-Imam Allah in a Wolofised version meaning the guide for Allah. This is one of the titles of the prophet Muhammad. Libasse Chaw did not officially become Limamou Laye until he proclaimed his mission, yet there are stories that attest to his special qualities as a boy and young man. Thus when we are speaking of Libasse Chaw according to the historical record, we use Libasse Chaw. When referring to the hagiography and aura of Libasse Chaw, we use the name Limamou Laye.

Childhood

Libasse Chaw was born in 1843-4 to Assane Chaw and Coumba Ndoye. Both parents come from Lebu families who had been on the

Cap-Vert Peninsula for centuries. Assan Chaw was a fisherman as was his father and his father's father. Most Lebu men were fishermen who supplemented their income with agriculture.

Libasse Chaw was given the name Limamou because of a prophecy his father and other Lebu men received from Sheikh Ahmadou Hamat Ba also known as Mouhamadou Ba or Limamou of Ouro-Mahdi. Ouro Mahdi was Mouhamadou Ba's village located in Fouta Toro which is in northern part of present-day Senegal. Mouhamadou Ba was a very well known and respected Islamic leader. He declared himself to be the Mahdi or re-newer of Islam for Fouta Toro in 1828. He is also remembered for publicly sacrificing an infant son in order to "prove his faith." Another of his sons, probably the oldest, Ahamdu Ba known popularly as Ahmadou Sheku, led a jihad in the Kingdom of Jolof in 1869. We have already discussed Ahmadou Sheku's jihad in chapter two.[1]

Assane Chaw and other Lebu went to Ouro-Mahdi to benefit from Mouhamadou Ba's *baraka*. Mouhamadou Ba told them that the Mahdi would be born among the Lebu and that his name would be Limamou. Mouhamadou Ba told them to name their sons born in the next few years as Limamou. Limamou is the Wolofised version of the Arabic al-Imam. According to the oral record, fourteen Lebu boys were named Limamou after the prophecy was given. Of those fourteen boys, Libasse Chaw was the only one who survived until adulthood. Obviously this adds to the mystique and miraculous aura surrounding Limamou Laye. In reading the hagiography, we do not seek for truth. The important matter here is what is believed to be true as well as who believes it. While doing field research, all subjects pointed to this story and the following account as unassailable reasons supporting Limamou Laye's claim to be the Mahdi and the reincarnation of the prophet.

One of Libasse Chaw's childhood friend, Tafsir Ibrahima Mbengue, recounted how when they were children they were surprised by a group of angels who immobilized Mbengue and picked Chaw up in the air holding him suspended while they opened his chest put some things inside and closed it again. Mbengue says that Libasse Chaw told him to keep that a secret. Mbengue complied until after Limamou died.[2]

It is important that the Layenne adherents hinge much of their belief on the two stories above. Using Weber's definition of charisma as a contract between the leader and the people based upon the leader's ability to do certain things. In examining Limamou Laye's charisma we must analyze what it is based on. In this case, it's not the ability, but his status. One doesn't become a prophet overnight. If we look at the record of prophets in the Judeo–Christian–Islamic traditions, the greatest ones always have a noteworthy childhood. Moses was miraculously rescued from infanticide. Jeremiah was to the office of prophet from his mother's womb. Jesus was born of a virgin and confounded intellectuals at the tender age of 12. On seeing an adolescent Muhammad, the Christian monk Bahira proclaimed that he would be the prophet that followed Jesus. Libasse Chaw cannot become Limamou Laye. He had to have been Limamou Laye all the while, just hidden from most people. The above mention stories make him Limamou Laye before he proclaimed his mission at age 40.

In an interview with Serigne Mbacké Laye, Limamou Laye's great-grandson, he recounted another story. Limamou was play-fighting with his friends. As they were playing at different intervals the friends would stop playing and call out to him. After several instances of this, the young Limamou asked them why they were doing this. One friend responded, "The first time I called you, your feet were deep in the ground way below the surface. The second time, your head was far above the clouds." The young Limamou Laye warned the whole group not to tell anyone what they had seen.[3]

Serigne Mbacké told another tale not popularly known. In this instance, Limamou was sick. He dug himself a hole in the sand, sat in the hole, and refused to eat anything except the grains of millet that fell as people passed and/or winnowed their millet. *Borom tuur* and *ndokpat* were called in to heal him. When they prepared to do their sacrifices, the wind would come and blow the sacrifices away. In the end a powerful marabout was called in to treat an obvious emotional malady. The marabout arrived to see the young Limamou sitting in the sand chanting "laye laye, Muhammad a rassulallah, laye laye." The marabout looked at the young Limamou and wrote "Muhammad a rassul allah" in the sand next to Limamou and then went in the house to talk to Limamou's mother. Limamou, miraculously cured, got up and joined his mother and the marabout in the house.[4]

The first story similar to the one that Mbengue told essentially points to the supernatural nature of a young Limamou Laye. The second story, however, is more relevant to a particular part of Limamou Laye's mission: the fight against the traditional religion. There are several stories that tell of Limamou showing himself more powerful than the traditional religions after he proclaimed his mission. However, the story above portrays his spiritual superiority even as a child. The message of superiority goes beyond one person. With the appearance of the Muslim marabout it becomes apparent that Limamou is part of a larger force which supersedes all other spiritual forces and sources. Islam is proclaimed as greater than the feeble traditional religion. Limamou is not only seen as a mere part of this greater spiritual force, When the marabout writes "Muhammad a rassoul Allah" he is proclaiming the Layenne assertion that Limamou is the reincarnation of the prophet Muhammad, thus he is God's Imam. He is at the pinnacle of the spiritual pantheon of Islam. The only one above Muhammad is God. Considered apostasy by some, this assertion is believed my tens of thousands and forms the foundation of Limamou Laye's charisma.

What does it take for a person to believe these stories? Answering this question is difficult at best seeing that all of our informants were 2nd and or 3rd generation Layennes. Looking at the larger picture, however, Libasse Chaw was an illiterate fisherman among hundreds of illiterate fishermen. He had no immediately outstanding spiritual or physical qualities that might have put him above the others of his age and class. In order to understand why anyone would have believed him, we should take a look at Lebu history and society in the mid-19th century.

As we already noted in the last chapter, French colonization was suddenly and brusquely accomplished on 25 May 1857. The Lebou, who had been collecting taxes from the French during the previous 40 years, were busy celebrating the end of Ramadan and did not react thinking that their friends, the French, had only come to wish them a happy celebration. Once the French refused to pay their annual tribute, the Lebou understood what had taken place.[5]

Libasse Chaw was approximately 13 years old at the time. Not yet a man, but well on his way to manhood, he had to have understood at least parenthetically. Contrary to what Assane Sylla stated about the French's pacific attitude towards the Lebu, the French colonial structure appropriated land from the Lebu for the building of Dakar, Rufisque, and Thies. As Dakar grew, more land was appropriated. The Lebu were displaced to worse land. Their way of life was encumbered by French colonial expansion. They refused to send their children to the schools run by the French Roman Catholic missionaries. Poverty began to increase among them as some of their activities of trade were decreased because of French colonial expansion. Previously the Lebu had been the middlemen between the French on Goree and the hinterland. Once the French conquered Ndakaru and founded their capital Dakar, the Lebu lost a large portion of their trade.

Libasse Chaw had plenty of people looking for a savior in such an environment and willing to believe the unbelievable. There was another broader and longer conflict that troubled Lebu existence. This was the unavoidable and larger conflict between Islam and anything Islamic. There were Islamic scholars among the Lebu from the earliest times of their Islamization. In Islam, the doctrine of *jáhiliyáh* is the necessity of all Muslims to establish a break between them and an unredeemable pagan past. Many Islamic leaders used the troubles connected with colonization and those that plagued the country side during the 19th century jihads as proof that Allah was angry with the non Muslims and the Muslims who tolerated them.

Throughout the past two decades, analyses of Islam in Senegambia always begin with colonization. Though mentioned in passing, the long history of Islam in the region does not formulate a vital part of such analyses. There seems to be a consensus on the idea that Islam spread at the end of the 19th century because of the disturbances and uncertainties brought on through conquest and colonization. This reasoning cannot be shed easily because it just sounds reasonable. When we take into consideration the long history of Islam, however, we see that Islam had been progressing gradually over approximately 10 centuries in Senegambia. This progress was usually tempered and often hampered by monarchs and aristocrats, many of whom proclaimed themselves as Muslims. Colonization eliminated this tempering and hampering through conquest of these governments.

As stated above, the Colonizers never proclaimed war on Islam. They did, however, fight anything that possibly posed an obstacle or threat to the expansion of colonial power. Christian, Muslims, and traditionalists were persecuted at various junctures throughout the European empires if anyone from these groups seemed to be using their religion as a base for challenging colonial hegemony. Framing their disgust and protest locally, many indigenous African scholars (among them Khadim Mbacké who we quoted above) see their personal persecution as paramount while neglecting to contextualize it in the larger experience of the colonized.

Colonization was a threatening and potentially deadly force that created more problems than it solved and destroyed more than it built. Much has been written about the destructive force of colonization and her granddaughter globalization. The Islam v indigenous structure, however has suffered adequate analysis and has actually been subordinated in the whole schema of the analytical work. I posit that this conflict was more of a weight on Limamou than the troubles of colonization. Cecile Laborde asserts that Limamou Laye's mission should be interpreted through the vise of colonial *bouleversement.* On the contrary the process of interpretation is more complex. The Muslim interpretation of the colonial interruption was one of punitive action from Allah. Some interpreted it as punishment for those who refused Islam. Others saw it as punishment for those who hampered the progress of Islam. When Albuuri Njiye (Ndiaye) was under assault from the French, for example, he approached Sheikh Ahmadou Bamba for aid. According to oral tradition the conversation went as such: Albuuri Ndiaye told Sheikh Ahmadou Bamba, "I will fight against the *toubab*[6] who don't pray and I will be your Ali-Samba."[7] Sheikh Ahmadou Bamba then responded, "I know that Allah sent the *toubab* in order to bring peace to the country. You will get men killed for nothing, whereas, if they live, they will convert to Islam. If, however, you are bent on fighting, you will find in the East a warrior *marabout* [El-Hajj Omar Tall]. You have only to join up with him."[8]

Colonization was just a stimulus to which Islam had an answer. The traditional power structure and/or religion did not have any response on record. Judging from the reaction of the majority, the traditional response, if any, was not adequate. Most people began to reaffirm their Islamic faith. Thus it is inadequate to simply explain the all of this as a response to colonization without taking into account the wider conflict between Islam and the traditional religion. A more accurate description of the conflict would actually be one between the Muslims who held a purist position and Muslims who saw no harm in the adapted native traditions. The Islamic doctrine of *jāhiliyáh* was prominent in the Islamic texts so members of the *ulama* were usually the ones of the more purist position. There is also another Islamic doctrine of *taqíyah* which permits the believer to amend some of the articles of faith when performing those articles could be harmful to the Muslim or his/her community. The Jakhanke and other more peaceful clerisies obviously operated under *taqiyah* when living under non-Islamic rulers. The 19th century found the majority of the peoples of the Senegambia Islamized, particularly the Wolof, Fulbe, Mandingo, and the Lebu. *Taqiyah* was no longer a necessity. As the jihad phase which started with Nasr al-Din in the 16th century and did not wind down until the late 19th century plainly shows, there was a conflict between not only Muslims and non-Muslims but also more between Muslim purists and the more lax Muslims. Understanding the upsurge of Islamic turuq and reaffirmation of the Islamic faith during the second half of the 19th century requires that we move away from a simple assertion of colonization in our analysis.

Islamic scholars in Africa use the Friday sermons as a platform and often supplement it with open air preaching in getting their message out to the common people. With the two ideas having gone beyond the provenance of scholarly debate, the Muslims were faced with the choice. Unlike the Wolof, the Lebu actually had a vibrant indigenous religion among them. Thus the conflict was two dimensional with Islam versus the indigenous beliefs as well as Muslim purists versus adaptive Muslims. The above story involving young Limamou and the marabout bring this conflict into perspective. Within this context we see that colonization's role in the whole matter was not as important as scholars have made it. The wider conflict has been underemphasized and in most cases ignored. Colonization was a phenomenon that needed an adequate explanation. The purists offered the same explanation that they offered for the epidemics and the famines that occurred before conquest and colonization, i.e. God was punishing the unbelievers and the lax Muslims. Though both of his parents were reportedly illiterate, Limamou Laye's family was devoutly Muslim. Coming from such a family, when faced with the specter of a very real and long-lasting punishment in French colonial conquest, Limamou Laye chose the Islamic purist position.

Young Adulthood

Like most young Lebu men of the 19th century, Libasse Chaw became a fisherman. The fishing season runs from December to June. The rainy season starts in June which is also the start of the planting season. Fishing was closely aligned to the traditional cult. Prior to the founding of the theocratic republic, there was an office in the Lebu government whose job was to insure that the rab/tuur were appeased so that the fish would bite. This government position did not disappear after Jaal Joop took over, it was just incorporated into another position and lost much of its stature. The point here is that the important relationship between the tuur/rab and the fishing occupation was still a feature of Lebu society.

In Lebu cosmology there are rab/tuur that live in the ocean and they must be appeased. The ocean to the north of the peninsula is masculine and called *guedji oat*. The ocean to the south of the peninsula is called *guedji gi* and is considered feminine. When the two seas get together for sex, a tempest sets in. It is believed that eventually these two will eventually join and it will be the end of the world. When certain types of fish are rare in the ocean or the fish aren't really biting, one explains that the sea is angry with the fishermen. The sea is also believed to contain numerous mysterious creatures and water spirits who have great powers. One informant told of a friend's husband who when coming from the then new cinema (ca 1960's) in Dakar was approached by two young beautiful women. The two women called out to him inviting him to come with them. He followed them basking in their sensuality only to discover he was up to his shoulders in seawater. One woman insisted that he continue, but he refused. The other woman came out of the water and invited him to a house on land where she gave him the best dinner and best sexual experience of his life. When he awoke he was abandoned on the beach and his family had been searching for him for two days.[9]

Devout Muslims often go to the sea to pray and offer sacrifices of millet and other food stuffs to the water goddess. There are countless other myths and traditions centered around fishermen and water spirits. We can only speculate as to the extent to which Libasse Chaw involved himself with the cult rituals surrounding his profession. The hagiographical record, as can be expected, is silent on this issue. Judging from his later career, however, Libasse Chaw's involvement with such rituals was cursory if there was any involvement at all.

According to the oral record, Limamou Laye was generous to a fault. His family would rush to meet him when he arrived after a fishing expedition in order to get the fish before he gave it all away. His mother was known for her saintliness and devotion to Islam. She was also known for her charitable practices. When Limamou was a boy he invited all the poor people he could find to come and partake of the dinner his mother prepared.

While a fisherman, Limamou Laye is said to have been a part of more miracles. As a fisherman, his work often took him up and/or down the coast. While in Banjul, according to Cherno (Thierno) Sarr, one of Limamou's fishing companions, an old mystic by the name of Kebe Mansali approached the group and asked for help for splitting wood. Limamou volunteered. Mansali allowed Limamou to walk ahead of him. Once they arrived at Mansali's house, he offered Limamou a plate saying "Eat, this is the work I wanted done. I've discovered what I sought. Each night I've seen a light over the cabin where you and the other men sleep. The light follows you out to the sea each day. I saw it again over you when I let you walk in front of me. Limamou you should know that God is going to give you a prophetic mission prolonging that of Muhammad. Limamou, you're going to shake up the world." Limamou was so emotional he couldn't eat. Sarr says that after Limamou returned he told him that there was wood to be split at Mansali's place. Sarr went and Mansali offered him the same plate. After eating a bit, Mansali told Sarr that Limamou would be declare his mission one month and 10 days from that point. Cherno (Thierno) Sarr returned to Yoff and waited for the appointed time.[10]

This story is very similar to the story alluded to above about Muhammad and the Christian monk Bahira. Bahira encountered the caravan along which an adolescent Muhammad traveled with his uncle. It was Muhammad's first voyage. The caravan rested close to Bahira's home. Bahira saw a cloud that shaded the caravan. He noticed that the cloud left the caravan and followed Muhammad to where he sat under a tree. Though the caravan had passed Bahira's place many times before, he had never invited them to dinner. He invited them on this day to their surprise. While at dinner, he expressed an interest in Muhammad and proclaimed that he would be the prophet that was to follow Jesus.[11]

Sarr's story about Limamou shares too many points with the story about Muhammad. Both happen while the two men were traveling professionally. Both happened while the men were in the company of colleagues. Both tap into the force of an established and recognized personage of spiritual authority. The intent is to capture the attention of would be adherents by tying an established spiritual authority to a particular spiritual leader. In the case of Muhammad, the Christians are urged to accept his message since one of their esteemed monks attested to the validity of Muhammad and his message. In the case of Limamou, it is the Muslims of the area. They are urged to accept Limamou's claims as true since an established Muslim mystic has declared it so.

The Announcement

Sometimes during his young adulthood, Libasse Chaw took two wives Fatima and Farma. He had six sons, some of whom were born after he declared his mission. The number of daughters is unknown. Like most people of Senegambia, he was surrounded by a large extended family from the paternal and maternal lines. Libasse's mother died during his 40th year. His reaction was one of immense grief. He entered into his house, and for several days did not eat or speak to anyone. On the 24 May 1883, he emerged from his self-imposed isolation. He told his paternal aunt Adama Chaw, "O auntie, cover me with 2 white cloths and know that God has given you a nephew like none other in this world!" He then turned to his cousin Ndiaye Chaw and said "O my cousin cover me with new cloth and know that God has given you a cousin like none other in this world!" When he came out to the others, he was wearing three white pieces of cloth. One covered his head, the second his shoulders and midriff, and the third his waist and legs. He told his wives, "O chaste Fatima and virtuous Farma, God has given you a husband like none other in this world. The old Limamou that you knew is no more. God has done what he wanted. He has placed me over all creatures and charged me with the mission of calling all to submit to Him."[12]

Then he walked through his hometown of Yoff proclaiming his mission as a Mahdi stating "Ajibou da iyallah (listen to God's call)." People began to say he was crazy or possessed of a demon. He replied,

> "I am not crazy. I am the messenger of God sent to you. I bring you greetings. He who follows my recommendations will drink the divine liquors in the flower gardens of paradise. But woe unto those who doubt my mission and my title of Mahdi, me Limamou."[13]

This of course caused a stir in the community. His family was horrified from shame of the whole situation. People ridiculed him and by extension the whole family. Assuming that he was possessed by some contrary spirit or sick from the grief of losing his mother, the family prevailed on him to seek help. When one of his uncles approached him on behalf of the family to cure him, Limamou replied, "Only God can cure me. Only He knows who it is that is inside of me . . ."[14]

Limamou Laye's in-laws also thought he was insane and unworthy of their daughters. Both the wives' families recalled them home thereby nullifying the marriages. In traditional Senegambian family structure, the marital contract is always in danger of dissolution depending on actions of either party involved. Being that the marriage is between families and not individuals, the family of either the bride or groom also retains the right to dissolve the marriage. Marriages can be dissolved if the woman cannot deliver a child or if the husband mistreats the wife. Marriages can also be dissolved if some defect is found in either spouse after the marriage. Limamou's insanity was apparent to his in-laws and they dissolved the marriages on those grounds. Fatima, however, defied her parents and family and went back to her husband.[15]

Initially everyone thought Limamou was insane, but with time he gained a following and his fame for producing miracles spread even outside the confines of the Lebu territory. People came from all over the Senegambia region as his fame spread far and wide. His first convert was Momar Bineta Samb. According to tradition, from the beginning he came to protect Limamou. There were those who would have done him some harm. After announcing his mission, Limamou praised and glorified Allah all night and all day, publicly and privately. In Senegalese society, there is a certain amount of latitude shown towards the mentally ill. Sometimes children publicly ridicule the mentally ill, but in general people tolerate them as long as their behavior does not cause any physical harm to others. There are individuals with short tempers who, much to the consternation of the wider society, will physically attack the mentally ill, particularly when they make a lot of noise or do something, though not harmful, may be particularly disturbing. Certain types of behavior, however, can signal the punishment of the whole community.[16] Limamou's claims to be the reincarnation of Muhammad may not have bothered most Lebu people. However, Limamou launched a public relations campaign against the rab/tuur and their cult practitioners. To be sure there were those who saw his behavior as inviting punishment for the whole community. Momar Samb was the first convert and bodyguard.

Cherno Sarr Chom, the second convert, wanted to follow Limamou, but his family was strongly against it. Cherno left his house pretending to go on an errand to another village. He turned towards Limamou's compound where Momar Samb standing guard, moved to let Cherno Chom pass. Once inside, Cherno gave Limamou a very nice boubou.[17] Limamou told him "Ah Cherno, you came. It is sure that God is not slack concerning his promises." Then Limamou took off his white clothing and told Cherno, "You are the first person to give me clothing since I announced my mission. I will soon give you something that no other person can possess." According to the oral tradition, Cherno Chom saw the four angels who came and gave Limamou the spiritual credentials to announce his mission on a grander scale.[18]

The stories collected for the hagiography seem to have a running theme. Obviously the theme is to portray the mystical grandeur of Limamou Laye. The stories that involve particular individuals seem to grant special recognition to the source of such stories. Mbengue's story of the spiritual heart-transplant grants Mbengue special status as the only witness to this scene who repeated it only after Limamou Laye was no longer alive to deny or corroborate it. Sarr's story gives him special status as the only one to whom Limamou told what happened with Mansali. Sarr also shared in the miraculous revelation by eating of the plate that was previously offered to Limamou afterwards receiving the specifics of the prophecy, details of which were not even given to Limamou. Chom's son says his father saw the angels thus receiving the blessing that no one else would have that Limamou promised him. The collection of such stories took place after Limamou and his tariqa really took off. Obviously there were some who wanted to ride the tide with the Layenne leadership which is restricted to direct male descendants of Limamou Laye. These stories however, are major parts of the hagiography because they do not skip the mission of hagiographical accounts which is to attest to the saintliness of the subject.

Power is organized along a patronage system in Senegal. Sufism was particularly compatible with such a system. In Sufism a sheikh's spiritual power or *baraka* is at the disposal of his disciples. The closer one was to the sheikh the larger portion of the baraka was at his disposal. Baraka translates into influence, respect, and economic enrichment. The creation of a story that could heighten one's baraka is easy to understand.

The Duality of the Mission

We must distinguish between the two claims of Limamou Laye. Limamou said he was the Mahdi and as such he was the reincarnation of Muhammad. His claim of being the Mahdi was not extraordinary. Around the same time, Muhammad ibn Ahmad of Sudan proclaimed his mission as Mahdi. A few decades later Muhammad Jummat Imman would proclaim his mission as Mahdi-messiah to the Yoruba of present-day Nigeria.[19] As stated above in Senegal the 19th century jihadist, Sheikh Ahamadu Ba's father had proclaimed himself Mahdi decades before Limamou Laye.[20] In 1930, Serigne Abdoulaye Yakhine Joop proclaimed himself to be the Mahdi.[21] These are just a few of the Mahdist claims made throughout sub-Saharan Africa. Limamou Laye's proclamation of being the reincarnation of the Prophet Muhammad stands out against the tide of mahdist claims throughout the world.

Orthodox Islamic theology leaves no room for reincarnation of any kind. However, the Shia have a tradition of the rightly guided caliph reappearing at certain times. The Sunni idea of the Mahdi is different. There are some sects who believe in the coming of the Mahdi, who is supposed to renew the religion and recreate the golden age of Islam. Throughout the world during the centuries since Muhammad's death, men have proclaimed that they were the Mahdi. In the 9th century Abu Dawud recounted a tradition in his collection of Hadith that called for a re-newer of Islam at the beginning of every century. In the 15th century, Muhammad ibn Abd al-Karim Al-Maghili and Jalal al-Din Al-Suyuti, both Islamic scholars, propagated the idea throughout the Islamic communities of Africa. Al-Suyuti never visited sub-Saharan Africa but his ideas spread first to the Tuareg and then through the Tuareg. He also concentrated on a single re-newer in his eschatological writings, but did not deny the possibility of more than one re-newer coming before the end of time. Al-Maghili traveled and taught throughout what is modern-day Nigeria. Both of these scholars recognized that there were some problems in Islamic practice and education. They attacked this and proclaimed that there had been and will be reformers. Al-Maghili specifically gave a number of reformers. He also allowed for reformers in the various areas of Islamic practice and theology hoping that he would be considered a reformer.[22]

In light of all this, Limamou's claim of being the Mahdi was no surprise. The claim of reincarnation however caused a problem. In spite of that, Limamou had five prominent Islamic scholars submit to his authority. These men used their considerable talents to support Limamou's mission among the Senegalese ulama. We will now turn our attention to their efforts and the results.

Chapter 5

Limamou Laye and His Mission

After proclaiming his mission, Limamou Laye endured the consternation of his family and community. This was because no one believed in the mission of an uneducated man from a humble background. He did not distinguish himself before declaring his mission. However, his persistence in proclaiming his mission resulted in followers first among the Lebu and then from the wider region. His charisma was acquired through his rising spiritual capital. Spiritual capital is earned among the Lebu through the successful manipulation of public discourse. The traditional Lebu universe interprets everything in the natural world as a manifestation and/or a result of occurrences in the physical world. If fishing was bad, the water spirits were angry. If the crops did not yield the expected amount, the rab/tuur needed to be appeased. Thus the popular assumption was that Limamou proclaimed himself to be the Mahdi because he was possessed of evil spirits. Amid this level of opposition, the task of convincing the populace seemed at first glance immensely daunting and near impossible. The presence of Islam for centuries among the Lebu, however, had made them aware of Islamic traditions, including that of the *Imam al-Mahdi* and other eschatological predictions. A complicating aspect of Limamou's claim was his insistence that he was the second-coming of the Prophet Muhammad. As a result, his task of convincing the people took on another dimension. Who or what the Mahdi would be is not clear in the tradition, but it is clear that no one else had made the claim that the Mahdi and Muhammad were one and the same. The claim of a Mahdi could not, however, be ignored in any Muslim community as it forms a major part of the canonical hadith's eschatological imagery.

The Mahdi

The tradition of the Mahdi is an old one in Islamic history. Two traditions of the Mahdi can be identified in the Islamic world and both have numerous variations on the two main themes. The first tradition is that of the *shiah attu Ali* or the partisans of Ali known today as the *Shia* or *Shiites*. The Shia came together as a group after the murder of the fourth caliph, Ali ibn Abi Talib who was the cousin and son-in-law of the prophet Muhammad. Ali was the closest living male relative of Muhammad at the time of the prophet's death. Many thought Ali should have been the immediate successor, but Abu Bakr was the successor. A remnant of the early Muslim community held hopes of seeing Ali at the helm and were satisfied with his election after the murder of Uthman, the third caliph, in 656. Ali's rule was not universally accepted for, among other reasons, his unwillingness to condemn the murder of Uthman. In 661, Ali was murdered, his son Hassan was bought off and retired to a quiet life in the wake of Muawiyya's (661-80) ascension as caliph. After the death of Muawiyya in 680, another of Ali's sons, Hussein, answering the calls of Ali's supporters in Kufa, marches to them in Iraq. The supporters in Kufa withdraw their support after receiving threats of retaliation from the government. Hussein persists, thinking that the sight of the prophet's family marching would stir Islamic piety and urge people to his aide. Traveling with his wives and children along with followers from Medina, Hussein (holding his infant son) and his entourage were surrounded on the plain of Kaerbala in Iraq and massacred. This was a seminal event in the development of Shiism: . . .his death took on the aura of martyrdom. Karbala developed into the holiest shrine of Shiism, and the annual rites of mourning for Husayn at that site became the most important religious ceremony in the Shia calendar. . . . Husayn's martyrdom thus solidified the Shias belief that the individuals most qualified to hold supreme political authority over the Islamic community were the descendants of the Prophet through the line of Ali and his wife, Fatima, the Prophet's daughter.[1]

The Shia doctrine "evolved in the decades after Husayn's martyrdom," during which time the Shia developed as a distinct group with their own imams and evolved into an esoteric group who were driven underground during the reign of the Abbasids (754-1258). With a new concentration on the esoteric and the greater repression, the principles and beliefs of the Shia were kept secret for fear of being misunderstood by those who were not mystically inclined (such as the ulama who doubted the religious validity of the esoteric groups) as well as their political oppressors. Jaffar as-Saddiq, the fifth imam of the Shia taught this doctrine of taqiyyah to his followers. The Shia considered their imams to be religious leaders of the highest order, anointed and divinely-inspired and as such infallible. With this in mind the idea of *al-Mahdi*, or the rightly guided one, was consistently expressed in Shia theological conceptualization.

A more radically esoteric ideology emerged after Caliph al-Mutawakkil summoned the tenth Shia imam, Ali al-Hadi, to Samara and placed the Imam under house arrest. Wanting to deprive the Shia of their leader as a means of weakening the movement, the Abbasid government wanted to end contact between the Shia and their imam who communicated with their faithful through agents. After the death of the eleventh Imam, Hassan al-Askari, in 874, rumor circulated that he left behind a son who hid himself for protection from the Abbasid and other enemies. This hidden twelfth imam was never seen and communicated with the faithful through a succession of agents over the next 70 years. In 974, the hidden imam's agent issued a statement saying the imam would no longer be in contact with the faithful because God had concealed him and he was thus in occultation. The last message, however, said the hidden Imam would reappear before the end of the world to champion the just and true members of the faithful thereby establishing a reign of truth and justice. An offshoot Shia group called the Twelvers withdrew from political life waiting for the reappearance of the twelfth imam. According to the Twelvers, no government can be legitimate until the Hidden Imam reappears. The Hidden Imam is the Shia expression of al-Mahdi.[2]

The Sunni Mahdi is also a messianic figure but derives from folk legend probably grafted from Shia beliefs. Many of the Mahdist claims involve the Prophet Issa (Jesus Christ). The central idea of the Mahdi involved Issa and *Dajjal* or the anti-Christ. At the end Dajjal will arise and the Mahdi will challenge him and with the help of Issa ibn Mariama will kill Dajjal. This eschatological episode is not cited in the Quran but is recorded with several varying details in collections of *Hadith* and the writings of scholars.

The *mujaddid*, or re-newer, is another eschatological tradition that is often mentioned in conjunction with or mixed in the general Mahdi tradition. In the 9th century Abu Dawud recounted a tradition in his collection of *Hadith* that called for a re-newer of Islam at the beginning of every century. The Mahdi is sometimes recounted as the last mujaddid before the end of the world. Sometimes the Mahdi appears as a recurring re-newer within himself. The mujaddid however is of a lower status than that of the Mahdi. When asked if he were the Mahdi, Uthman dan Fodio did not aspire to such a great title but his son, Muhummad Bello did consider his father a mujaddid.[3]

In the 15th century, Muhammad ibn Abd al-Karim Al-Maghili (1425-1505) and Jalal al-Din Al-Suyuti (1445-1505) both Islamic scholars propagated the idea of the Mahdi and the mujaddid throughout the Islamic communities of Africa. Al-Suyuti never visited sub-Saharan Africa but his ideas spread first to the Tuareg of the Sahara and then through the Tuareg to western Africa. Also, many West Africans stopped on their way to Mecca and studied under al-Suyuti at his base in Cairo at the University of Al-Azhar, the oldest university in the Muslim world. Among those west Africans who studied under Al-Suyuti, the most famous one was Askia Muhammad the Great (1492-1528). Al-Suyuti propagated the idea of many re-newers of Islam, one coming each century. The final re-newer was to be the Mahdi. This idea dispersed and took other forms throughout West Africa.[4]

Al-Maghili traveled and taught throughout what is modern-day Nigeria, Niger, and Mali. Both al-Maghili and al-Suyuti recognized that there were some problems in Islamic practice and education. They attacked this and proclaimed that there had been and will be reformers. Al-Maghili specifically gave a number of reformers. He also allowed for reformers in the various areas of Islamic practice and theology hoping that he would be considered a reformer.[5]

Mahdism in West Africa

The 19th century (14th century of the Hegira) saw a surge in Islamic activist expansion in West Africa. Many, who had bought into the idea of the Mahdi or the rightly guided one of the faith, were awaiting the Mahdi. The most famous Mahdist movement in Africa is the Mahdiyya of Sudan (1881-5). There were many other Mahdist proclamations throughout West Africa. There was a significant Mahdist movement in Nigeria.[6] Some sources claim that Mamadou Lamine of northern Senegal proclaimed himself to be the Mahdi in the 19th century.[7] Mamadou Lamine's father did proclaim himself the Mahdi in the mid 19th century.[8] Followers of El Hajj Umar Taal, Uthman dan Fodio, and Ahmadou Lobbo, three of the most famous jihad leaders of the 19th century, considered them each to be the Mahdi.[9]

Many studies have made much of the fact that these Mahdist claims came in the 19th century during European conquest. The prevailing idea is that European colonization was the cause of the upsurge in Mahdist claims. Most of the studies of the Mahdi of Sudan present this view. As already mentioned, Laborde names French colonization as the direct cause of the Mahdist claims of Limamou Laye. Paul Lovejoy and J.S. Hogendorn's study on "revolutionary madhism" exhibited in the Mahdist uprising of 1905-6 in Northern Nigeria/Niger, while acknowledging that Mahdism can exist outside the context of colonial conquest, strips even revolutionary Mahdism of its history and major purpose as an Islamic eschatological tradition as opposed to merely a response to colonization with the study's focus on colonization. The fact that this revolt crossed the border into the French colony of Niger points more to the importance of it being a universally accepted Islamic tradition. The revolution named the traditional Islamic authority and the British colonial authority as enemies because they were seeking an otherworldly authority.[10]

In his study of the Yoruba Mahdi, Peter B. Clarke couches his analysis in the long history of Mahdism in West Africa, yet his analysis causal factors point to the disruption of Yoruba life perpetrated by the British colonial government. Muhammad Umar, however, counters this approach through looking at the continuum of precolonial Mahdist claims through post-colonial Mahdist claims.[11] Mahdism is an Islamic eschatological tradition which has appeared from early times until the present. The conditions of the Ummah being in a difficult position and the integrity of Islam suffering can be argued in each instance of Mahdism. Thus colonization created conditions as other events in the history of Islamic communities throughout the world had. An overwhelming concentration on Mahdism as a response specifically to colonization and not as an Islamic response to all challenging times distorts Mahdism, morphing it into resistance as opposed to the eschatological tradition that it is. As we have already attempted to conceptualize the surge of Islam in 19th century Senegambia as the culmination of nine centuries of gradual Islamic expansion to which colonization was an almost accidental catalyst, it is also essential to point out that Mahdism was an Islamic response to difficult times and not something specifically reserved for resistance to colonization. Accordingly, we can view the importance of Limamou's mission as not essentially a response to colonization, but only incidentally so. More pointedly, Limamou's claim seems to be aimed at a malaise within the Lebu Islamic community particularly the worship of the rab/tuur by Muslims seeking divine help. As interpreted by his hagiographers and in his sermons, Limamou Laye seemed to be more concerned with the purist practice of Islam thus fulfilling the role of *Imam al-Mahdi* prescribed in the various recorded traditions.

Limamou appropriated the tools of public discourse in order to lead the Lebu to an alternate explanation of his proclamations. Convincing the masses was no easy feat, but a more complicated group, the Senegalese ulama, remained obstinate in their opposition. The ulama of Senegal included the learned leaders of mosques, respected masters of various subjects within the Islamic sciences, and Sufi sheikhs. In the 19th century all the learned men in Senegambia came from clerisies or individual families with long genealogies some of which claimed the prophet Muhammad as an ancestor. Limamou was an illiterate fisherman without pedigree. He soon had defenders from among the ulama who had become his disciples. Consequently we can identify a two pronged defensive against his detractors. One involved debunking the spiritual authority of the *ndopkat* (agents of the traditional cult) and *boroom tuur* (traditional priests). The other was the use of religious rationalization in order to substantiate Limamou's mission.

Limamou and Muslims

As stated above, the idea of the Mahdi has a long history in Islam. The Sunni version of the Mahdi idea came to sub-Saharan Africa early and was propagated widely. Limamou's claims, however, seemed to combine elements of the Sunni and Shi'a ideas of the Mahdi. The acceptance of a Mahdi, however, was not difficult for an orthodox Muslim. The complicating claim of reincarnation was bravely explained away by a group of five Islamic scholars who accepted Limamou Laye's proclamation early in his mission. Assane Sylla, writing from an Arabic version of Limamou Laye's biography written by Mokhtar Lô takes the time to list these five scholars and their specialties. Most of them were experts in Quranic exegesis, and all were fluent in Quranic Arabic. Tafsir Njalanda Geuye was the imam of the big mosque of Rufisque. After becoming a disciple of Limamou Laye he elicited the consternation of his fellow *ulama* and was eventually forced to give up his position as imam. Tafsir Abdou Gaye became Limamou's personal secretary writing all his correspondence. All the correspondence from Limamou to the French colonial authorities was written by Abdou Gaye. Tafsir. Abdoulaye Jallow was an interpreter with the French colonial administration. He submitted to Limamou Laye and was imprisoned with him on Goree. Tafsir Jibreel Gaye, an eminent scholar, also converted. Mokhtar Lô is also counted among the first of the Islamic scholars converted to Limamou Laye's mission. Other learned scholars answered Limamou's call and believed in his mission. Among them was Ababacar Sylla, who had served for 22 years as the Imam of the Grand Mosque in Dakar and the judge (*cadi)* of the Islamic Tribunal of Dakar. When the other learned Islamic leaders of Dakar heard of this, they openly renounced his decision. He resigned his posts in Dakar and went to serve Limamou Laye.[12] Others joined at the risk of being disowned by their families.

The ulama responded with an emphatic opposition to the mission of Limamou Laye. Those among them who chose to follow Limamou were initially castigated and ostracized. There is no record of other Sufi sheikhs coming out against him and his mission. Sheikh Ahmadou Bamba Mbacké sent a delegation of his followers to Limamou

Laye's funeral instructing them to be respectful because Limamou was a true man of God. The other Sufi sheikhs did not send people to the funeral and seemed on the whole to ignore Limamou Laye and his tariqa.

Efforts were made by the above mentioned scholars, particularly Mokhtar Lô, to validate Limamou's mission. Assane Sylla is an anthropologist and a Layenne. His father was an Islamic scholar who answered the call to Limamou Laye. Assane Sylla translated Lô's hagiography into French, as mentioned above. Sylla also translated Limamou Laye's sermons, which were recorded in Arabic by Abdou Gaye. Assane Sylla authored a book on Limamou Laye's dealing with the French government, a useful study which combines oral tradition with a study of the archival record.

Sylla continues the efforts to validate Limamou Laye's mission through the Quran and *Hadith.* He makes a bold claim for the coming of the Mahdi based on the *Hadith.*[13] The Quran, however does not seem to provide any support for Sylla's argument of the theological validity of Limamou Laye's claim to be the reincarnation of the Prophet Muhammad. In his volume entitled *Le Mahdi Seydina Limamou Laye: soleil de l'Occident,* Sylla bravely appropriates Quranic verses in his attempt to build a case of Muhammad's reappearance on earth before the end of time.

There are different collections of Hadith, which Sylla uses to support Limamou's claims. Some Hadith are reportedly discounted by various authorities. Since Islam does not have one unique authority comparable to the Roman Catholic pope or the various Orthodox patriarchs who can or cannot definitively establish the validity of the Hadith, different collections of Hadith are believed and supported by different groups, while others are discounted. The various Sufi turuq have their leaders who make certain decisions about what is acceptable and what is not. Then there is the orthodox scholarly community, the ulama, which formulates their opinion often in opposition of the various Sufi leaders. Amid these caveats, it is difficult to assert definitively that Limamou's claims are "un-Islamic." The diffusion of real power in the Ummah makes this possible as long as Limamou Laye's followers follow the basic tenets of Islam.

Ousmane Mbengue makes a bolder argument for the mentioning of the Mahdi in the Quran although most scholars agree that it is not mentioned there. According to Mbengue the Quran cannot be taken at face value because God revealed it using parables which require intelligence to interpret. He then takes verses from the Quran using them out of context to support Limamou Laye's mission. For example he cites the verse from Surat Al-Jumah (62) verse 2, "He is the One who sent to the gentiles a messenger from among them . . ." Mbengue cuts the verse off there. The rest of the verse reads, ", to recite to them His revelations, purify them, and teach them the scripture and wisdom. Before this, they had gone far astray." It is clear that the Quran was talking about Muhammad. This type of Quranic 'exegesis' is a classic case of grasping at straws. The ulama remains unconvinced.

Khadim Mbacke states that the Senegalese ulama does not accept the claims of Limamou Laye. Surat Al-Azhab verse 40, reads "Muhammad is not the father of any of your men, but the Apostle of God and the seal of the prophets." Citing this scripture Khadim Mbacke discounts the possibility that any prophet can be born after Muhammad which in essence means that no other ethnicities on the earth will be blessed with a prophet. He continues, "The ulama also rejects the idea of incarnation and considers it to be foreign to Islam." Mbacke seems to imply that Limamou Laye could possibly be a reformer since he did reform Islamic teaching among the Lebu citing the Hadith compiled by Abu Dawud. His final statement on the issue, however, is negative. "The Senegalese ulama have not been insensitive to the desire of Limamou Laye to reform those Lebu customs and traditions that are contrary to Islam. However, they cannot admit a doctrinal reform that flies in the face of a fundamental Quranic teaching about the finality of prophecy with Muhammad. Yet the theoretical rejection of what they consider to be a heresy has not been translated into practical opposition to the Layenne movement."[14] Khadim Mbacké published his book in 1995, thus it is obvious that the efforts of Mokhtar Lô, Assane Sylla, and Ousmane Mbengue over three generations have not won over the Senegalese ulama.

Acquiring Symbolic Capital: Limamou and the Traditional Religion

Every emerging leader must have a public relations strategy to acquire the necessary charisma, or as David Robinson terms it, symbolic capital, which is also the term I prefer.[15] Unlike other Islamic leaders of this time, Limamou Laye did not have the familial standing among the learned Islamic families of the region. Neither had he attained a personal reputation as a scholar. So from where would he get his symbolic capital? Most of Limamou Laye's fame spread from miracles.

The traditional religious leaders, the *boroom tuur* and *ndopkat,* as discussed in chapter two, are responsible for intervening in the spiritual world on behalf of their adherents in order to affect real change in the physical world. The most common request was the healing of sickness. Illness in the Lebu universe is the result of a something going awry in the spiritual world, thus the boroom tuur and/or ndopkat were sought for help in solving the problem. Ideally, the diagnoses included identifying something someone has done to upset a balance in the spiritual world. Once identified, rituals were performed to right the wrongs. Many times illnesses were not successfully treated in this manner. The popular confidence in the boroom tuur and ndopkat was so potent that when it was seen that an ill person could not be cured through the spiritual means, all hope was lost.

Limamou Laye launched a public relations campaign against the leaders of the traditional religion. He had to face the Lebu's strong belief in the healing power of their genies. Even the Muslims appealed to the genies when they were gravely ill. His first attack was verbally denouncing the power of the rab/tuur and their practitioners. Then he went a step further when successfully healing those who the boroom tuur could not. One of the most recorded miracles is his ability to make people fall as if dead, and then make them rise at his will. He drove demons away, and awakened the dead on at least one occasion.[16]

Mokhtar Lô recounts one could even hear the demons crying in agony refusing to give their identity.[17] This reads like a page from the

Bible, when Jesus cured those possessed of demons.[18] The power of these statements takes us back to the Lebu understanding of the world in which the spirit world and physical world have a symbiotic relationship. The power to affect change in the physical world through the spiritual world is the basis of the charisma among the Lebu. Limamou Laye exhibited this power and thus established his charisma.

Limamou's charisma exhibited a profound potency when a group of his followers destroyed the sacred rock of the village Mpal. In Lebu traditional religion, the rab/tuur (divine spirits) live in trees, rocks, and bodies of water. Once a spirit takes up residence in a particular place, that place becomes sacred to the adept. Mame Kantar was the spirit that lived in this sacred rock and she was the protector spirit of Mpal. The population of Mpal was aroused by the sacrilegious act.[19] This did not endear Limamou and his followers to the Lebu power structure or the French Colonial government which would complicate things for Limamou later.

Layenne Theology

The Layenne literati, seeking to downplay the importance of the Lebu religion, have often stated that the traditional religion was not a religion at all. They assert that the Lebu were thoroughly Islamized but practiced rituals of the rab/tuur alongside Islam. The Lebu were Islamized by the 19th century, but the traditional practices did constitute a religion. They have a belief system, ritual action, sacred space, and active engagement with a defined spiritual reality. Muslims and Christians alike tend to take the condescending view that African traditional religions are not religions at all. Animism, fetishism and other derogatory words were used throughout the colonial period to describe indigenous religions from around the world. The Layenne writers have taken this line from the manual on Euro-supremacist reasoning, endowed it with missionary zeal and spiritual purpose, and repackaged it as history. The end result is Islamic-supremacy that seeks to denigrate anything that is not Islamic or Islamic enough. The problem with any ideology whose premise is to prove the inferiority of others is that the premier example of "the superior" changes arbitrarily depending on who is articulating the supremacist ideology. In the case of the Layennes, the Senegalese ulama denigrates the Layennes using the same line of reasoning. The French Colonial government, in turn denigrates the whole of Black Africa's Islam as not being pure or Islamic enough using the same line of reasoning. Like the layers of an onion, we can peel away the various layers of this superior/inferior ideology only to find emptiness. The originating kernel of the whole ideology is the Arabic chauvinism that complicates Islam.

The Quran declares that Muhammad was a prophet for all nations. Yet he appeared to Arabs first and established the religion's liturgy in the Arab tongue thereby creating the sacra-sanctity of the Arab language and culture. Limamou Laye's proclamation that he was the Mahdi (and as such the reincarnation of Muhammad) has been opposed theologically without actually examining the larger implications of such a proclamation. According to unpublished documentation of the oral record, Limamou Laye proclaimed, "The Prophet Muhammad who slept is now awaken. The Arab has become black."[20] If Limamou Laye is to be believed, the Wolof language is as good as the Arab language for transmitting God's word, the Lebu are as just as much a chosen people as the Arabs are, and thus by extension Yoff and Camberene (Layenne spiritual centers) are as good as places for pilgrimage as are Mecca and Medina. There is no record of Limamou Laye ever making a pilgrimage. Of course the European colonial governments limited the number of people who could travel, thus the once large stream of Muslim pilgrims slowed to a trickle during the colonial period. Muslims created sacred spaces within their grasp to which they made pilgrimages. To be sure, this practice of localizing sacred space did not originate during the colonial period, but it took on a different meaning. The circumstances forced people to cling more resolutely to the local sacred places. Yet the construction of Touba as the sainted place for Murides and the designation of Yoff and Camberene as the pilgrimage place for Layennes takes on a more significant role because these two turuq are local to Senegal. With the Layennes, the significance shifts on the pivotal assertion that "the Arab has become black." Then all the areas that constitute the sacred personality of the "Arab" have also become black, but not to the exclusion of the "Arab."

The implications of such a claim were too onerous for the orthodox Muslims and more specifically the ulama. They knew that they cannot publicly and totally discount Limamou Laye because of the record of his miracles and, as Khadim Mbacké pointed out, his insistence on strict adherence to Islamic orthodox practices. Yet his claim of being the reincarnated prophet questions one of the essential assumptions of Islam, that the last prophet was limited to the Arabs only.

In the face of Arab chauvinism which pervades the Muslim world, many African Islamic leaders turned to what Sheikh Anta Joop terms "sherifism" or the creation of genealogy proclaiming descent from the prophet Muhammad. Sheikh Anta praises Sheikh Ahmadou Bamba Mbacké, founder of the Murridiyya, for not succumbing to sherifism and for establishing local shrines tor which adherents could make affordable pilgrimages.[21] Obviously unknown to or unrecognized by Sheikh Anta, Limamou Laye did the same thing. Sheikh Ahmadou Bamba never claimed descent from the Prophet Muhammad, but his relatives do.[22] Limamou Laye's relatives, on the other hand, have not succumbed to "sherifism." They exemplify their spiritual kinship to Muhammad's family, but they in no way, claim physical relationship. Quite the contrary, they proclaim their Blackness and their Lebu origin proudly.

In a world where some believe that God only speaks in Arabic, Limamou Laye was a threat to everything sacred. If we examine Limamou Laye's claims in the light of the Sunnah and the Quran, we see no explicit denial of the possibility. Limamou Laye never discounts that Muhammad is the seal of the prophet. On the contrary if he did discount the notion of Muhammad being the last prophet, he could have just named himself Limamou the prophet to the Lebu. Saying he is the reincarnation of the prophet Muhammad allies his mission with the world renowned sacred Islamic tradition and ties that sacred mission to the Lebu in particular.

For too long, scholars have ignored the psychosocial impact that the implication of Arab chauvinism can have on the non-Arab adherent. For a proud people, the issue has to be resolved before Islam can integrate into the host society. Lamine Sanneh asserts the turning point in the spread of Christianity in Africa came when the scriptures were translated into native languages.[23] Islamic scholars have established the consensus centuries ago that the Quran would lose something in translation and should remain in the sacred language of the original revelation. Though there are Qurans in translation today, it is a relatively new innovation with the first being translated into English in the early 20th century. How did Islam survive this impasse in Africa?

Sufism eased the spread of Islam in Africa. Jamil Abun-Nasr argues that Sufism's worldwide appeal can be explained by the fact that it provides a religious leadership structure where the temporal leadership had fallen short. Muhammad had occupied both roles but after his death religious leadership suffered as contenders fought for the leadership role.[24] In the African context, Sufism offers a leadership structure comparable to the priest hierarchy of traditional African religions. The traditional African religions, which often had orders that one could attain and a clear distinction between the adherent and the clergy, seemed to be closer to Sufism, which has a wird (sacred repetitions usually taken from Quranic verses) and levels of esoteric knowledge that one can attain in order to become a sheikh.

Sufism as a conduit for Islam appealed to African spirituality with the concentration on esoteric knowledge. The African worldview is comprised of a cosmological understanding in which there is a spirit world that mirrors the physical world. The spirit world and the physical world run parallel intersecting at certain points in a human's life, i.e. dreams, death, birth, and religious experience. The powerful person is one who contains a spiritual knowledge which enables him/her to work through the spiritual world to affect change in the physical world. African spirituality also exhibits itself in the form of spirit possession. The ecstatic behavior seen in African-American Christianity is comparable to the ecstatic dancing and spirit possession seen in African traditional religions. Scholars have sufficiently argued this point for decades.[25] Some Sufis in Senegal have all night dances with drums, a reminiscent of the pre-Islamic dancing.[26] African spirituality expects this type of spiritual/physical interaction regardless of the religious context. Thus Sufism provided an attractive form of Islam in which the African can be him/herself.

Most importantly, Sufism provides a leader, the Sufi sheikh, who was one in a chain that connected the adherent to Muhammad. Al-Tijani proclaimed himself the imam of Muhammad. Sheikh Ahmadu Bamba Mbacke declared that he was the *khadim a rassoul* or servant of the Prophet. Limamou Laye went beyond them all declaring that he was the Prophet reincarnated especially for the Lebu people. Muhammad ceased to be an abstract historical figure with a foreign language and culture. Muhammad became part of the Lebu family. In this manner, Limamou Laye and his followers "lebuized" Islam. The Layennes developed a theology based on and rooted in a traditional Lebu concept of reincarnation.[27] Lebu concept of reincarnation includes the idea that a child can come and be born and die over and over again as punishment to the parents/society for some breach of protocol in their worship of the ancestors. This dead child can be a dishonored rab or a tuur or some other malevolent spirit. Whatever its identity, the spirit returns to the earth in order to right some wrong.

In the Layenne belief system, Muhammad came back to the world because a wrong was being committed: the infection of Islam with Lebu traditional practices and beliefs. In this case however, the baby carrying the spirit did not die. His life was necessary to right this wrong of the community. When Limamou Laye stated "The Prophet Muhammad who slept has awoken, the Arab has become Black," he put the Prophet Muhammad in the ancestry, making him eligible to be an ancestral spirit. In this regard, it is accurate to state that Limamou Laye challenged the ideology of Arab superiority on which Islam was founded.

Here we must turn to his sermons in order to gain insight to the fundamentals of his theology. From his available sermons, we see a great effort to endorse orthodox Islamic practices. This is one of the major stated goals of his mission. The Lebu had already had a form of Islam for over two hundred years, but, as stated above, their version of Islam was syncretic at best. Getting them into orthodox Islam could only strengthen his position. Contrary to what some Senegalese Muslims believe, Limamou Laye did not try to start a new religion. For his assumption of the image of the Mahdi and the reincarnation of Muhammad, he needed Muslims.

On the other hand, the fact that most of the Muslims did not practice Islam exclusively was also to his benefit. In an orthodox Islamic community with a strong cadre of scholars, Limamou Laye's claim of Mahdi could not be predicated on another claim to be the prophet Muhammad. While in a community of believers only in the traditional religion, he would not have been able to attract much of a following without first converting people to Islam. Thus the background of the Lebu was fertile soil for the type of mission that Limamou Laye developed.[28]

In short his theology was one of orthodox Islam, modified only to fit his proclamation of being the reincarnation of the Prophet Muhammad. There was also a stressing of the idea that the end of the world is near. Living in an era where the traditional leadership and native rights were being constantly eroded and replaced with French hegemony, an eschatological theology had a natural appeal. The apocalyptic nature of Islam cannot be understated, but in each sermon, Limamou Laye uses graphic imagery to compel his listeners to conform their lives to the laws of Islam because the end is near.[29]

Limamou Laye and the French

As Limamou's following grew, he attracted the attention of the French. After having fought many leaders of violent jihad in West Africa, the French were nervously aware of any new Islamic leader who garnered a huge following. Some colonial officials had been watching the Layennes and considered them harmless. Cleret, an over-zealous minor official, however, was certain that Limamou Laye was a threat to French interests in the region and he convinced his superiors of this.

Cleret had informants among the Lebu who did not like Limamou and wanted him gone. He had upset the natural order of things with his preaching and his miracles. He had challenged the traditional cult leaders and antagonized scores of Muslims with his proclamation. According to the report of his followers, Limamou's congregation actively participated in the life of the community. If anyone was sick and needed his fields planted or harvested, the village men would all contribute time to the task. Limamou and his followers worked alongside their village brethren in this task. During the Islamic holiday, Aid el Kebir, or Tabaski for the Wolof, Limamou would share his mutton with people from all turuq (Islamic brotherhoods or Sufi organizations), most notably the leaders of the Tidjanniya as well as the political and social leaders of the Lebu. He actively participated in the fishing and agricultural activities of his congregation.[30] Through this example and his miracles, his following continued to grow.

Yet the Lebu leadership did not take to Limamou Laye and his people. The relationship which eventually became cordial was nasty at the beginning. Serigne Mbacké Laye plainly said the Lebu government conspired with the French in order to have Limamou arrested. Among the Layenne informants, this seems to be an acknowledged fact. The French do mention the name of a Lebu official who informed them against Limamou Laye. The alliance between indigenous government officials and Islamic leaders also happened to Sheikh Ahmadou Bamba Mbacké. It is obvious that once the indigenous rulers saw that the maintenance of their power lie in the hands of the French, they made friends with the French. The people however saw their power as illegitimate and seemed to flock to those whose power was disconnected from that of the invaders. Sheikh Ahamadu Bamba provided such a power initially. Before he died however, the French eclipsed his temporal power with two exiles and a house arrest.

With the Lebu, the situation was different. The Lebu chiefs kept their power and were only required to collect taxes for the French and serve as intermediaries between the Lebu and the French colonial government. The Wolof kings were stripped of all their power and reduced to the role of a simple chief. The Lebu had always been a minority people surrounded by greater empires and governments. They had once paid tribute to the Kingdom of Cayor and were now paying to the French. Though much of their land was taken, the disruption of their everyday lives occurred gradually enough so as not to create a catastrophic situation as it did with the Wolof when their governments were destroyed.

The Lebu leaders, however, did not look kindly on any challenges to their power. Under the Wolof kingdoms, marabouts were allowed to exert influence and build up large followings as long as they did not pose a direct challenge to the temporal power. As a theocratic government, the Lebu government saw Limamou Laye's power as a challenge to their temporal and their spiritual supremacy. He had to be eliminated and they did everything within their power, though covertly according to sources, to be rid of him. The archival sources do not speak to this specifically though the name of one Lebu detractor is found in the colonial government's correspondence. The oral tradition, however, is very clear on the enmity between Limamou Laye and the Lebu government.

"Three Years, Three Days, and Three Months"

In 1886, the French became aware of Limamou Laye and his followers. Reported to be already at 300, from his sources, Cleret, the director of the interior, sent a letter dated 17 December 1886 to Baginski, head of the interior at Dakar, stating that Limamou and his followers were a potential threat and should be under surveillance. Baginski responds by sending a secret agent, Mbaye, to approach the Limamou as a convert in order to spy. Sarr says Limamou knew all along that Mbaye was a spy, but allowed him and his partner to stay.[31]

Mbaye stayed with the Layennes for some time and wrote a one-paged report describing no illicit anti-French teaching or any other breach of security. On the contrary Mbaye reports that Limamou seems preoccupied with assuring that his followers "cultivate their fields of millet, marry and take good care of their wives, and practice Islam strictly constantly singing of the uniqueness of God."[32]

The alarm of a French colonial government still trying to subdue Samori Toure (1882-98) who was described as the Napoleon of west Africa, was far from complete. The conquest of the interior of Senegal would not be soothed with one report. Continued surveillance witnessed the addition of disciples from all parts of the colony of Senegal. In a letter dated 4 September 1887, Cleret told the interim governor of Senegal, Quintrie that Limamou's followers had already reached 5000. Fueled with claims that Limamou Laye was purchasing arms in preparation for a holy war against the French, on 7 September 1887, the colonial officials sent 10 gendarmes and their chief, Huguenin to arrest Limamou Laye.

According to El Hajji Malik Sarr and Assane Sylla, the rest went on as follows. The gendarmes find a 10 year old Seydina Issa (named for Prophet Issa ibn Mariama or Jesus Christ to Christians) Laye in the courtyard and ask him where his father is. Seydina Issa replies that he was inside the house. Limamou, who was doing his ablutions in preparation for prayer, pretended not to hear them and continued his ablutions. The French gendarmes thinking Limamou had fled set fire to his roof. Limamou touched the roof saying "Asbiyallahou!" (in the name of Allah) and the fire went out immediately. Huguenin then aimed his pistol at Limamou who turns his ear toward the gendarme saying "make sure you aim well at this ear so you can kill me." Huguenin tries to fire but it will not go off. Limamou then raises his shirt and says "aim here well." Again the pistol would not fire. Huguenin then comes forward with handcuffs and claps them on Limamou Laye who compliantly says "make sure they're closed good and tightly." Then Limamou says a few words and the handcuffs pop off his wrists. Exasperated, the Huguenin runs toward Limamou to attack him. Limamou blows on the gendarme who then falls paralyzed as if dead and Limamou goes on to the mosque to lead the prayer accompanied by his followers. After a few hours, Limamou and his disciples return. Limamou comes and stands in front of the prostrated gendarme, recites a few Quranic verses and says "Get up, you miserable fellow, you are not worthy to die in the yard of men of God." The gendarme follows the example of his subordinates and runs leaving behind his handcuffs and pistol.[33]

Knowing that this was not the end, Limamou called his disciples together and told them that he would soon be leaving Yoff because the French were coming to arrest him. Not wanting to bring any negative affects upon his disciples, Limamou Laye sent them back to their homes and prepared his family and close followers to abandon his home. On his exile he had his trusted disciples Abdoulaye Jallow and Cherno (Thierno) Sarr.[34]

Leaving in the wake of a French force bent on arresting him, Limamou Laye made his *hijra* to Guéntaba northeast of Yoff along the coast, which would become the site of Camberene, a Layenne village. Before coming to Camberene, Limamou and the three disciples who followed him stopped to pray at a site along the seashore that was later named Jaamalaye meaning "peace of God" in Wolof. Today Jaamalaye is the site of Limamou's son and successor, Seydina Issa Rohou Laye's mausoleum and is the destination of an annual pilgrimage for the Layennes.[35] Eventually Limamou Laye was arrested and exiled to Gorée Island on 14 September 1887 for three months.[36]

During the exile, the fledgling community benefited from the able leadership of Limamou's top lieutenants who reminded them of his words of encouragement. Once released, Limamou and his growing sect encountered numerous accusations and persecutions at the hands of the native officials who served the French. This only drew the community closer, which resulted in the creation of a new Islamic identity for the group. Although illiterate, Limamou strongly encouraged his disciples to learn Arabic. He led the way by sending his sons to study under the noted scholar, Tafsir Ibrahim Mbengue. Limamou Laye also established a camp for his Wolof followers many of whom had come from different parts of Senegambia. The camp was located at Guéntaba which is now called Kem Medina, meaning like Medina, or commonly called Camberene. It was called such since it was the terminus of Limamou's *hijra* like Medina was for the Prophet Muhammad. Today most of the inhabitants of Camberene are descended from the original Wolof settlers. Though the Layenne tariqa evolved from a Lebu cultural base and worldview, Limamou Laye's power was effectively broadcasted to the Wolof regions. Many people came to see him. According to the reports from indigenous and French colonial sources, the crowds were exceptionally great. We hesitate to quote numbers because both sources have a tendency and motive (though different) to exaggerate the numbers.

Shortcomings of the Movement

We have already identified what drew so many people to Limamou Laye, but we have not examined possible reasons why many people did not stay with Limamou Laye. As previously mentioned, the Wolof kingdoms had experienced pronounced conquest and colonization. Many of those who previously had power, particularly the ceddo, were suddenly powerless. The ceddo were a class of soldiers who fought for the crown and received booty from their battles. Technically slaves of the crown, they lived in luxury enjoying European products (particularly whiskey) and riches acquired from capturing and selling slaves. Oftentimes these slaves were stolen from among the free peasant population. Peasants began seeking refuge in the Islamic villages which had greater autonomy and a measure of security from the raids of the ceddo. Once the precolonial governmental structure was destroyed, the organized state terror perpetrated by the ceddo ceased. Thus the ceddo power ceased. Many former ceddo were seeking a leader, a way to regroup. Some reportedly went to Sheikh Ahmadou Bamba's tariqa. Some also came to the Layennes. Since the French had shown that they possessed a greater temporal power, some of the Wolofs were looking for an exhibition of power beyond the grasp of French hegemonic forces. The esoteric source of power was what they sought. To the ceddo who lived in the presence of Muslim intellectuals of the court as well as the Muslim chiefs of Cayor who often banded together against ceddo encroachments, the sight of an illiterate fisherman would not have been as imposing or impressive as a renown scholar surrounded by scores of students working, reading, and writing such as Sheikh Ahmadou Bamba. One of the major services of the Muslim leaders in Senegal was and is the making of amulets or *gris-gris* to protect one of potential harm. Making gris-gris involves writing as Quranic scriptures are copied on small pieces of paper and sewn up tight in leather or cloth pouches. Limamou Laye could not write and thus did not make gris-gris. He lost esteem in the eyes of those coming from other parts of Senegambia for whom writing was an essential part of being a Muslim spiritual authority.

Others could not accept Limamou's claim of being the Prophet Muhammad reincarnated. As stated above, this was too much for most Muslims to accept. Though Islam had been among the Lebu for more than 5 centuries, it had been among the other Wolof for 9 centuries. Those who lived in areas where Islam had been institutionalized were bound to have a more thorough grounding in orthodox

Islamic understanding. Judging just by the detailed Mahdist tradition in Senegambia along with the centuries old community of scholars, a populace of Muslims would have developed a concretized concept of what is and is not allowed in Islam. Since reincarnation of the prophet does not figure at all in the written religious discourse of the region, the likelihood of many from the other Wolof areas accepting Limamou's claims were slim.

Another obstacle to the rapid expansion of Layenne beliefs among the Wolof are the Lebu features of Layenne practice and belief that appeared foreign to the Muslims of the Wolof kingdoms. The Layennes sing for long periods of time (around 10 minutes) before each prayer five times each day. The singing is ecstatic and also takes places before all religious ceremonies. Limamou commanded this singing in order for the congregants to distance themselves spiritually from Satan and all order of evil thoughts, in other words, to prepare the heart for prayer through worship. Reminiscent of the traditional religious musical summoning of spirits, the singing oftentimes result in spirit possession but usually not at the prayer times.

The Layennes also allow women into the mosques, though in segregated quarters. Though this is not unique to the Layennes, in rural Senegal, the mosques were small and only men were allowed inside. The presence of women in the hallowed space is more than some men could handle. Women are prominent in the traditional Lebu religion often serving as priestesses. Limamou Laye strictly forbade his followers to participate in the traditional religions, but for women to not be allowed to perform their Islamic religious obligations was nonsense for Limamou.

Though not directly connected to the Lebu culture, the next three practices were also difficult for the Wolof to accept the marriage of all girls at birth and the circumcision on the eighth day after birth. Limamou Laye also commanded his followers to wash their hands up to the elbow and their feet up to the knee. The common practice is to wash the hands to the wrist and the feet to the ankle when performing ablutions. Limamou's new practices are often interpreted as *bid'ah* or innovation which is strictly condemned.[37] Though many believe that there are good innovations and bad innovations, some

Muslims do not involve themselves in such hair splitting. Limamou's claim of being reincarnated Prophet Muhammad, together with unorthodox practices created an ideological obstacle for many Wolof to become Layennes.

The Death of Limamou Laye

Seydina (prophet) Limamou Mahdiyou Laye died on November 4, 1909. He founded his tariqa 20 years earlier and led it unchallenged. Starting from scratch, Limamou Laye managed to overcome the obstacles of his humble family background and lack of formal education. His leadership skills are unmistakably sharp and a credit to his memory. However, the limited success of his movement's growth to other sectors of the population point to his goals. His legacy is unmistakably the establishment of an Islamic movement among the Lebu. Sylla and Sarr as well as others have shaped his legacy in terms of his role as prophet to the Lebu people.

Sarr goes further expanding the mission to one of a Black prophet for Black people. Sarr reports Limamou as having told his detractors of his native village Yoff,

> "Is it because I have black skin today that you don't want to recognize that I am the messenger of God, the Mahdi? You would all have believed me if I had white skin. Don't you know that my skin color is the work of God who wanted me to be black today? Who can color better than our sovereign Lord? Oh! My black brothers, our supreme master sends me to you in order to deliver you from evil. I bring you the word of God. Take advantage of my teachings and you will receive heaven as your reward."[38]

Sarr continues making an argument for Limamou as the first one to articulate the philosophy of *Negritude.* He argues "In effect, the Senegalese, see Africans of his époque, particularly the Wolof and the Lebu, are convinced of the inferiority of the black race. For them, the black can't be a messenger of God . . . Limamou showed the contrary proving that the black race is equally dignified to other races (if not more), that God . . . hasn't given one race privilege over another." He then goes on to cite a song that the Layennes sing

"He who doesn't like Libasse	*Kou bagne Libasse*
Dislikes someone greater	*Bagne nga koula guene*
The blacks are ungrateful	*Nitt kou gnoul dafa rey*
If he were white,	*Boudone nitt kou khess*
They would follow him"	*Gnou djappa dineme.*[39]

Citing Limamou's flight from his home in Yoff in the wake of a French force coming to arrest him, Sarr says that Limamou did this to avoid bloodshed knowing that his followers would fight before allowing their leader to be taken. Sarr goes on to say that "before Mahatma Ghandi, who was so young, found his voice or even knew his vocation, Limamou Mahdiyou Laye was already preaching that noble doctrine to which he is the grandfather: non-violence."[40]

While Sarr, writing in the 1960's, attempted to bring the role of Limamou into two major philosophical responses to racism and oppression, Sylla frames Limamou in the wider Islamic eschatological tradition through recounting the Hadith and the whole Mahdi tradition constantly pointing out "evidence" for the claims of Limamou as recounted above. What Seydina (prophet) Limamou Laye did leave as indisputable legacy was an Islamic tariqa among the Lebu with followers from among the Wolof. He created two Holy places as sites of annual pilgrimages: Yoff, his native village, and Camberene, a city he created for his followers who originated in other places. The Layennes with their placement close to the urban center of the capital of the AOF (Afrique occidentale francaise), had advantages and disadvantages. The existence of the Layenne tariqa would serve as a nice buffer organization between the colonial government and the Lebu people taking the place of the increasingly irrelevant Lebu government.

Chapter 6

Passing the Torch: Limamou Laye and Seydina Issa Rohou Laye

This chapter chronicles and analyzes the passage of power from Limamou Laye to his son Seydina Issa Rohou Laye. Limamou Laye founded the organization, and his personal charisma was the force behind the growth of the group. Seydina Issa Rohou Laye had a seemingly seamless (according to the sources) passage of power. Our focus is on how Limamou Laye's leadership paved the way for and was complimented by Seydina Issa Rohou Laye's leadership.

African Leadership and Lebu Leadership

In the analyses of present-day African leadership, scholars tend not to take into consideration the traditional forms of authority and leadership as precursors to the modern African leader. This is a weakness of other analyses that we wish to address in our analysis. Traditional African political authority was clearly defined and limited. Though much has been said about the uniqueness of the Lebu "republican" governmental structure with delineated power roles, West African monarchies were all limited in scope and reach concerning their authority. The Wolof monarchs were all chosen by an elective council, though they often had to validate their position by defeating challenging claimants on the battlefield. Once in position, these monarchs had various officials who held inviolable authority and aided in governing. The monarch's primary role was to serve as the head of state and a symbol of the unity of the state. Some of the other positions were hereditary or held by strongmen who had been in the office for a long time. Thus, the monarch's authority, though often broad, was limited.

Leadership styles evolved from within the limitations on the monarch. Depending on the personality, the leadership styles varied. Some commonalities of leadership styles, however, helped define authority for the Wolof. One of the major features of the prevailing leadership styles was the insistence on exaggerated deference by all subjects. Actually, this practice was more constitutional than a feature of style. If a leader was not shown such deference, his/her subjects would not respect him. We see vestiges of this in Africa today with political, religious, and traditional leaders.

Another common feature of Wolof leadership styles was the use of diplomacy in dealing with the conflicting power relationships within the realm. As there were features of federalism in the Wolof monarchies, there was a constant tug of war between the head of state and the powerful village chiefs as well as military commanders and other strongmen/women. The play for power was intricately elaborate and involved much intrigue, often resulting in violence. Once one of these under the monarch stepped out of line, punitive raids were carried out against his/her domains. Sometimes the result was a full-scale war as was the case in 1795, when the Islamic chiefs rebelled against the *dameel* (king) of Cayor's authority resulting in the Joop family seeking refuge among the Lebu and eventually ruling the Lebu. The times of violence, however, were last resorts once the use of diplomacy failed. The attempts to hold together the government of overlapping mandates of authority required Herculean efforts and keen diplomatic sense.

The Lebu government possessed more internal stability than the Wolof kingdoms, yet the Wolof traditional authority structures fed the formulation of Lebu government. The hierarchy of authority among the Lebu was ordered on much the same lines as that of the Wolof kingdoms. The representative government worked better for the Lebu because they were always a small grouping of villages, unlike the Wolof realms. As delineated in Chapter 2, the traditional Lebu authority structure consisted of specific officers whose roles were not overlapping or confusing. Deference was still paid to the officials and diplomacy was required, yet unlike in the Wolof kingdoms, there was no real issue of one official's actions threatening another's.

Another source feeding the formulation of Layenne power was the traditional sufi leadership structure. In Sufism, the authority emanates from an individual's esoteric knowledge/power exhibited in his/her actions. As leader, the individual is also expected to use his/her esoteric abilities to corral and aid his/her followers. With this in mind, the leader's *baraka* (power of blessing) is accessed through the followers' submission, meaning that in all matters esoteric and many practical choices (such as marriage, occupational choices, etc) the leader's decision or at least blessing is required. As mentioned earlier, Sufism was the major vehicle for the quick spread of Islam throughout West Africa. The Lebu were not exempt from membership in the sufi *turuq* (plural of tariqa or brotherhood). Most Lebu are members of the Tijani tariqa. Libasse Chaw was a member of the Khadre or Qadre tariqa. The significance of this is that the submission process informed the formulation of Layenne leadership as did the display of authority in the civil Lebu and Wolof governments. These influences explain the technical details of Layenne leadership but they do not explain the long-term appeal of Limamou Laye.

Charisma and Limamou Laye

Max Weber's explanation of charisma and its role in institution building though written nearly eighty years ago still is accepted as valid. Scholars of religion in Africa have also pondered how Weber's explanation fits with the reality of African religious leadership. In Christian Coulon and Donal Cruise O'Brien's edited volume *Charisma and Brotherhood in African Islam*, the introduction states that the leaders of the brotherhoods have "not quite charisma." In his introduction, Cruise O'Brien tries to link *baraka*, the Islamic concept of spiritual stature/blessings, to Weberian charisma. He terms *baraka* as NQC or "not quite charisma" because it is passable from father to son.[1] I take issue with this argument. Weberian charisma is simply the result of an unspoken contract between the authority and his constituency whereby, the constituency accepts the leader's authority based on the understanding that he/she possesses "specific gifts of the body and spirit" through which he/she can lead the followers to a better existence. If somehow the charismatic leader loses these special qualities or is proven not to have possessed them at all, he/she also loses his/her charisma. Weber goes on to say kingship evolves from charismatic authority.[2] Thus the concept of the "divine right of kings" emanates from some first king who established the charismatic authority. In much the same way, an Islamic sheikh's authority is based on his saintliness and his successors' authority emanates from the initial charismatic authority. With this definition, *baraka* cannot be simply tossed aside as "not quite charisma."

There is a bigger issue with Cruise O'Brien's introduction. The application of Weberian charisma, a conceptualization born of a Western framework, cannot be easily applied to an analysis of a tradition born and nourished distinctly outside and in many ways in opposition to the West. The concept of *baraka* is not particularly complex, but understanding it requires the ability to refer to not only a breadth of knowledge on esoteric Islamic representations but also how these representations were tweaked when they came into contact with traditional pre-Islamic societies. I am not suggesting that Cruise O'Brien, the doyen of Mouride studies, does not possess the knowledge to understand *baraka*. It is clear, however, that he avoids or is incapable of explaining *baraka* within the context of Islam in Africa as opposed to glossing over it in an incomplete analysis within a failed translation of a Western conceptualization of authority.

Limamou Laye possessed charisma, Weberian or otherwise. His followers then and now insist that he had special supernatural gifts that enabled him to mediate between them and the Almighty. Other contemporaries of Mame Limamou, like Cheikh Ahmadou Bamba Mbacké and other Sufi sheikhs who had come before all acquired a following based on *baraka* evidenced in their erudition, *kholwa* (voluntary seclusion where prayer, fasting, and meditation strengthen the saint), in addition to miracles. Limamou Laye's whole mission was based on his declaration that he was the reincarnation of Muhammad. In one perspective, he had very little to prove his assertion because the basis of his claim was couched in his own conceptualization of who the Prophet Muhammad was. Thus he could explain all his actions through that prism and the crowd accepted it. So without erudition and *kholwa*, what made Mame Limamou's claims believable? The miracles cited above were the anchor of his claims. In comparison with other leaders, Mame Limamou's evidence seems flimsy. However, we must again contextualize our analysis in the culture of those to whom Mame Limamou addressed his mission. African Spirituality involves a *gnosis* that often is in conflict with the epistemological concentrations. That Mame Limamou possessed esoteric erudition, trumps his illiteracy. That he devoted himself to strict observance of Islamic ritual surpasses him not practicing *kholwa*. Mame Limamou's spiritual powers translated into real benefits for his followers in the physical world; thus, his charisma's evidence was compelling to those who had watched their loved ones die from previously incurable diseases. For those displaced economically, socially, and politically caught in the early stages of globalization at the hands of French colonial authorities, Limamou gave them a localized center of power beyond the reaches of the great white colonial arm. How did this charisma transfer to Seydina Issa Rohou Laye upon the death of Mame Limamou? As the tariqa was young and small, Seydina Issa had to anchor his charisma in another grand claim.

Consolidating the Mission: Seydina Issa Rohou Laye and His Authority

Born in Yoff in 1876 to Seydina Limamou Laye and Fatimatou Mbengue, Seydina Issa Rohou Laye took the helm of the Layenne tariqa following his father's death in 1909. By all accounts, he was a quiet and studious child always obedient to his father. Early in his education, a miracle is recounted. Seydina Issa and Ibrahima Mbengue were sent to study under Njaga Gaye. Gaye charged the older Mbengue to teach Seydina Issa the letters of the Arabic alphabet. Each time he attempted to have Seydina Issa repeat after him, Seydina Issa would faint. Mbengue gave up saying "this child can't learn." Limamou Laye laid his hand on Seydina Issa's head and said three times "Issa will learn. He who is called to be the imam of the entire world must learn."[3]

Seydina Issa's childhood was relatively uneventful except for the arrest of his father, which disrupted the whole household. Around the age of 30 in 1906 or 07, however, Seydina Issa took issue with his father's choice of marriage for Seydina Issa's younger sister, Aida Sene Chaw. Seydina Issa was not consulted before the decision was made, much to his consternation. He replied by leaving his father's house and staying for some time with various followers of his father. Another version of this incident cites that Limamou Laye was not happy with Seydina Issa's response to the marital contract and invited Seydina Issa to leave the house. Sylla cites an underlying spiritual reason that two "lights cannot live in the same house."[4]

While on his own "exile" Seydina Issa stayed in Put at Mor Wade's, a prominent disciple of Mame Limamou. While away, Seydina Issa learned of his father's death in 1909. A month prior to hearing of his father's death, Seydina Issa had a vision at Ngahkam in which angels on horses were coming toward earth. By the time the earthly messengers had made it to Seydina Issa with the news, it was late and those in Camberene wanted to bury the body. Seydina Issa's younger brother Madione intervened saying "surely you will wait for my brother to come back before burying my father."

The older disciples listened to Madione and eventually Seydina Issa arrived by train. At the train station, there were Catholics awaiting the arrival of Jesus Christ in response to some prophesy. Seydina Issa was also 33 when his father died. It had already been proclaimed and was again asserted that Seydina Issa was the reincarnation of the prophet Issa/Jesus Christ who in Islamic eschatological tradition would come and help the Mahdi/Mujadin defeat Djaggal/anti-Christ. The powerful imagery anchored the charisma of Seydina Issa Rohou Laye and helped to ease the transition from an elder surrounded by disciples of similar age to the authority of a young man to whom the elders submitted without problems (at least no problems that were recorded in the written or oral records).

The oral tradition recorded in the works of Assane Sylla records Seydina Issa Rohou Laye as a strict no-nonsense leader. The rituals and regulations of Islam had to be observed in detail. If any breaches in conduct occurred, Seydina Issa had no problem reprimanding followers publicly. He is cited as having screamed at singers that they were perverting the worship when they were singing of him and his father and their exploits. When disciples would see him, they would often react violently with passionate emotion. "You get no blessings!" he told them. "You're screaming for nothing! Above all, sing for God and his prophet."[5]

Seydina Issa Rohou Laye is said to have possessed the power to communicate with spirits and had genies (jiin) at his command. He had a curfew and often circulated himself to enforce it. He always told his disciples not to go about at night as this was the time for beings "not of this world." One of his followers, Mbaye Diene, was returning late at night and a man accompanied him and began a conversation. Mbaye Diene was returning late from Dakar to Camberene on foot, a journey that takes around 30 minutes by car today provided there is no traffic. Diene says the man approached him and began to ask him questions about where he was going and why he was out so late alone. As they walked and the questions became more personal and the conversation more bizarre, Diene says he was really trying to find a way to get away from that man without being rude. Upon arriving close to his home, Diene says the man turned to the stranger and bade him farewell. The man gave Diene a cane and charged him to give it to his "master" and disappeared. Diene slept late the next morning, so Seydina Issa Rohou Laye sent for him. When he awoke, thinking maybe he had dreamed the whole thing, he went to see Seydina Issa. Seydina Issa greeted him and made some small talk and then asked for the cane. Diene was so afraid he nearly fainted. He then understood that Seydina Issa had sent the spirit to accompany Diene home knowing that he would have a long walk home alone at night.[6]

Sylla and other chroniclers of the Laye family betray a great concern with legitimizing their leaders' claims to the rest of the world. The story cited above of Christians awaiting Jesus on the day that Seydina Issa arrived was repeated in various interviews during the research stage of this project. Many of the stories are told only by one person or only written in one spot, thus the repetition of certain ones leads me to believe that there is a body of stories that forms the heart of the hagiography and is passed down to followers in their childhood. While discussing this with a Layenne, my hypothesis was confirmed. Like the *Hadith*, the stories are varied and some obscure. Certain ones are accepted by the group as a whole, particularly those who add support to the claims of al-Imamou al-Mahdiyou Lahi and his son Seydina Issa Rohou Lahi.[7]

Sylla published another similar story supporting the claims of both father and son. His book has photocopies of supporting documents for this story. Cherif Sakik, a descendant of Muhammad and imam in Medina, sent a package to Seydina Issa Rohou Laye. Seydina Issa had written to the Cherif earlier. When the Cherif received a party of Senegalese who had come for the *hajj*, he asked if anyone there knew Seydina Issa Rohou Laye. Among the pilgrims there was a Lebu who was not Layenne, Ibrahima Mbaye, who agreed to take the package to Seydina Issa. The significance of the package is that the inscription on it was written in Arabic "to the Seydina Issa Rohou Lahi, the son of the Imam of all Imams." Coming from a confirmed and widely accepted descendent of the prophet, this inscription held great importance. Assane Sylla records Mbaye's recognition of the surprise of other pilgrims upon hearing the Cherif ask someone to send a package to Seydina Issa, someone who most Senegalese Muslim leaders did not take seriously because of both his claims and those of his father. We have already seen this attitude in the comments of Khadim Mbacké cited above. Much was also made of the fact that Mbaye was not nor ever became a Layenne, so obviously it was not a big hoax created by overzealous Layennes.

Seydina Issa and the French

Mame Limamou Laye had an initially adverse relationship with the French colonial power. Once both sides realized that their interests did not conflict, a *modus vivendi* was achieved as it was with other Islamic leaders. David Robinson terms this relationship "accommodation." The French even relied on the Islamic leaders of their colonies to help rally people in times of need and in some cases to help in administration. The French even proclaimed themselves to the world as an Islamic power.

Seydina Issa continued the *modus vivendi* without much change, except that he is cited as having been vocal about the uncompensated seizure of land from the Lebu in particular and Senegalese in general. Often making the French uncomfortable with his remarks, Seydina Issa thought the French were eyeing his and his follower's prime oceanfront property as the Dakar metro area took shape. He made it plain that there would be no theft of his land and that he had not forgotten the earlier theft of land from his people. He actively advocated those whose land had been appropriated without compensation according to Sylla. There is no archival record of exactly what he did for those whose land had been stolen, but there is evidence that he petitioned for the creation of new villages where his followers were resettled.

One of the villages he created was Gossas for which he had to ask permission of the French commandant Boloncard and the Bour-Siine (traditional king of Siine) Kumba Ndoffen Joof for the land and permission. Of course he had to use his spiritual power to clear the land. The forest there was the home of genies (jiin), who were not to be disturbed. Seydina Issa effectively chased the genies with the right words and the workers heard the rustling and saw the wind sweep away the malevolent spirits. Then the workers cleared 5 km in 20 days. Three hundred and thirty disciples responded to the call of Seydina Issa Rohou Laye.

In 1914, there was an epidemic that raged in Dakar. Seydina Issa Rohou Laye had Camberene moved and burned the old city to help contain and destroy the illness. The French were very happy with his actions. The French seemed to view Seydina Issa as a progressive Muslim leader who never incited his followers against the French and often helped the French in the implementation of their policy. The building of the great mosque and mausoleum of Limamou Laye was a great feat for Seydina Issa Rohou Laye. David Robinson calls this situation accommodation. The term is accurate according to its denotation, but the connotation implies a hint of submission. When describing the relationship in his well-written study, Robinson does explain that both sides had to concede some things as well as accept concessions from the other side with the French conceding less. With Seydina Issa Rohou Laye, his concessions were few because the Lebou treaty with the French gave them a unique position. Furthermore, the Lebou villages became absorbed into urban Dakar (which was also once a Lebou village), and their cooperation was vital to the economic success of French colonization. With the advent of peanut cultivation in the Siine-Saloum "peanut" basin, the same could be said of the

Mourides and Tidjanis as they all contributed to the continuing cultivation. Thus, *la mission civilatrice* took a backseat to economic gain. Catholic priests were discouraged from establishing schools in the hinterland as they were in Algeria. In the early days of colonization, the Islamic schools were the main source of formal education for most natives in present-day Senegal. After the initial stage of suspicious persecution of Islamic leaders, the French realized that these leaders were not in opposition to them. As stated above, the Islamic reform movements were hampered by many precolonial kingdoms of present-day Senegal. The peace that the French brought and the dismantling of much of the traditional sociopolitical order enabled the progress of Islamic reform. Robinson does not emphasize this at all. This particular weakness of his analysis does not take away the importance of his work. Seydina Issa and other Islamic leaders went to France in 1931 to receive medals from the French for their participation in the betterment of Franco-African relations as well as the work surrounding the war effort. This is indicative of the relationship. The Africans were honored and rewarded, but they were brought to France to be on display as an example of the "good" of the French colonial effort, strengthening already onerous stereotypes of Blacks. The leaders certainly were not oblivious to the situation. The medals could have easily been awarded in Senegal as many were previously.

Seydina Issa was not adverse to the French or their overall mission in Senegal, but according to my sources, he held a suspended contempt for the French being polite because culture dictated it. There was most likely the lingering bad feeling connected with his father's treatment. There were, however, no recorded problems between Seydina Issa Rohou Laye and the French colonial government. The *modus Vivendi* held and the Layenne constituency expanded and enjoyed considerable influence with their French overlords. This was the situation when Seydina Issa Rohou Laye died in 1949 and his brother Madione became the leader of the tariqa.

Expansion of the Faithful

We will now turn from our narrative to explore the growth of the tariqa. The Layenne tariqa experienced much growth after the death of Mame Limamou. The biggest agent of growth from the tariqa seems to be reproduction. With the expansion of European medical treatment among the native population in the four communes (Dakar, Rufisque, St. Louis, and Goree), population growth occurred. The possibility of jobs and the development of urban Dakar also contributed to many leaving the interior and moving into the area covered by the Layennes. From the available sources, however, Layennism spread more through reproduction than converts. Cecile Laborde offers an explanation for the paucity of new converts in her analysis of the particularism of Mame Limamou's mission. He was a prophet sent to the Lebou, however the majority of the Layennes are Wolof, and most Lebu are Tidjanis. The original Wolof converts for whom Mame Limamou built Camberene multiplied quickly and passed the tariqa to their children.

Some changes did occur as the tariqa evolved from a new Islamic voice to an institution. The major emphasis on Mame Limamou being the reincarnation of Muhammad was not abandoned, but there was more emphasis placed on the message of a purified Islam. For many years as young Senegalese girls began to dress like young Westerners in jeans and miniskirts, it was understood that in Camberene this was unacceptable. As late as 2005, there were bands of young men with belts roaming the streets of Camberene to catch girls in jeans in order to whip them.[8] The hours of prayer are strictly observed in Camberene and Yoff. There is ten minutes of singing before each session of prayer, which is intended to get the adherents in the mood to worship and pray to Allah. Wednesday nights there are sessions in the yard of Sheriff Ousseynou Laye at which many young people come and sing. The singing goes on for around 45 minutes followed by a sermon after which other leaders in attendance often speak. The faithful then receive blessings and prayers from Cherif Ousseynou Laye. It resembles a Wednesday night Bible Study meeting at churches across America.

These types of cultic services, the insistence on a dress code for women, and the strict adherence to prayer all come together to produce an institutionalization of Layennism that gives birth to a regularization of a once named deviation in Senegalese Islam. This explains in many ways Khadim Mbacké's assertion that even though most Senegalese Muslims think of the Layennes as an aberrant group, they are not publicly persecuted or despised. The proliferation of the group's life and practices amongst the young also created a group ready to integrate the more radical ideas into the fabric of the Senegalese religious ideal. There is an active association of Layenne students who have worked to create the official website and who produced a pamphlet to explain the basic tenets of Mame Limamou's message. Have they netted any proselytes? No one could give me a clear answer on this. There is one former Mouride marabout who has switched his allegiance to the Layennes, but as for the average Muslim there does not seem to be a lot of changing at all, least of all to the Layennes. The young Layennes, however, also tend not to change over and as long as they are growing older, having children, and passing the beliefs to their children, the tariqa will not easily die.

Basis of Expansion

Throughout our discussion of Limamou Laye and his Layenne tariqa, we have mentioned here and there the forces that led to his tariqa and the composition of the Layenne theology and practice. Now we must pause in the narrative to critically analyze the basis of the birth and expansion of the tariqa. Over the last four decades, scholars have struggled to define syncretism and adequately how (or even if) it happens in the African context as Christianity and Islam are introduced and spread. Different scholars have posited various opinions about syncretism and the way it unfolds in the African religious evolution. Shorter states that syncretism is impossible without a constant exchange of ideas and meanings, that is, a dialogue. In other words, the traditional religion and the new religion must be involved in a negotiation requiring constant communication. Peel states that syncretism can only occur when theological concepts are exchanged or merged. Thus, nonreligious cultural practices can continue into a new religion. When talking about Christianity among the Yoruba, Peel says that the syncretism exists among those who practice Christianity and still retain faith and trust in the traditional religions without any problems with the obvious cognitive dissonance.[9]

Both Shorter and Peel were writing about Christianity in Africa. Because of the overabundance of mission church documents, the conversion experience and evolution of Christianity in Africa has been thoroughly studied. Islam however, has not had particular attention paid to the specific point of conversion and thus the development or avoidance of syncretism. Scholars who study the spread of Islam rely on patterns observed over centuries in the absence of documentation comparable to that of the Christian missionaries. Two of such scholars are Robert Horton and Humphrey Fisher.

Horton says the Africans possess a two-tiered cosmology comprised of the local gods and ancestor spirits on the first tier and they all concerned themselves with the local lives and events, or the microcosm. The supreme god on the second tier deals with the world as a whole, or the macrocosm. According to Horton the Africans' lives revolved around the local, but because of colonization and other events, their world was opened up to a larger world thus a greater concentration on the supreme god developed and Christianity and/or Islam was accepted because the world suddenly lay at their doorsteps.[10] If this is true the syncretism would be unavoidable at some point.

If we apply Horton's explanation to an analysis of the Lebu, it is clear why Islam took root early on. The Lebu lived on the coast and were in contact with Europeans from the 15th century on. They had come into contact with Islam prior to their migration to the Cap-Vert. As a migratory group, the realization that the world was wider than their small community was a part of their existence. Settling on the coast and coming into contact with Europeans as well as the other peoples they encountered, would have only strengthened this idea. Though traditional Lebu religion was portable in that the Spirits moved along with the people, the proclamation of the prophetic tradition in Islam emanating from the one creator was so potent, that explanations arose describing the tuur's response to Islam. Some are recounted as having converted. Thus, Horton's seems to fit the Lebu experience.

Fisher criticized Horton's model for being too narrowly based on evidence from Christian Africa, yet being applied to Islamic Africa too. Fisher identifies three stages of conversion in Islamic Africa: quarantine, mixing and reform. Quarantine refers to the era when clerisies or Islamic groups of any type move into a non-Islamic area and keep to themselves practicing their religion in peace with no overt effort to convert the surrounding peoples. Mixing occurs when some from the non-Islamic people go to the Muslims for help of some type (writing, charms/amulets, prayers, etc.), which establishes a contact that continues. Reform occurs once some Muslims rise in opposition to the syncretism around them and urge for pure Islamic practices to reign.[11] This model is a generalization of what happened throughout Islamic West Africa over centuries.

Jaal Joop's flight to the Lebu could easily fit into Fisher's model, except the quarantine stage did not really take place. Jaal Joop had matrilineal family connections and quickly found a place with his relations as partisans. He expanded certain positions in the traditional Lebu governmental institutions creating space for Islam while not excluding the pre-Islamic traditional space. Islam's arrival predated Jaal Joop's flight by centuries, thus his task was not particularly taxing. The Lebu had probably already proceeded through the earlier stages of Fisher's model.

James Searing tests both models in his study of conversion among the Safen Serer of Bandia. Searing chooses this grouping of Serrer who were conquered and dominated by the Wolof during the early colonial period. Their conversion to Islam seems to have evolved from the crisis of having to give young men to France's war effort during World War I. The maternal uncles having authority over their nephews submitted them as recruits to the Colonial Army. The nephews, in turn, saw it as betrayal and began to turn their back on the traditions in exchange for Islam, which supports a patrilineal power structure. Searing concludes that elements of Fisher's model as well as that of Horton are evident in the experience of the Serrer of Safen. The focus of Searing's study, however is on the conversions of individuals as opposed to the community's conversion. The Safen Serrer still have their traditional shrine and the guardian of the shrine proclaims himself a Muslim as does most of the village.[12]

Writing about the Wawa and the Kwanja of Cameroon, Quentin Gausset presents an example where the Wawa chose Islam and the Kwanja chose Christianity as a general rule. Gausset argues that both groups embraced new religions in the 1950's and 1960's in order to fit into the new modern state of Cameroon, which, in turn, fitted into a wider global community of nation-states. He further argues that their choices of one over the other were based on their relationship with the Fulbe, who came in the 19th century bringing Islam. The Fulbe joined with the Wawa in order to defeat the Banyo Sultanate while simultaneously raiding the Kwanja who fled in order to avoid enslavement. Gausset goes on to identify two definitions of conversion supported by the existing literature. The first definition is the changing of one's identity as opposed to actual practice. The second one is the changing of one's practice or what some scholars refer to as "real" conversion. Gausset also runs over the models proposed by Horton and Fisher as an attempt to bridge the two opposing definitions of conversion. Gausset seems to agree with the first definition of conversion though he recognizes those who seem to have undergone the second definition. He says the second definition seems to rest on fervor, which is difficult to observe objectively.[13]

Cecile Laborde in her study of the Layennes, insists on labeling them syncretic without actually explaining why. From the strands of opinions on conversion and syncretism, we lean toward the definition of syncretism given by Peel and the conversion model presented in Fisher's work. Thus, Laborde, cannot be right. Islam had been among the Lebu for centuries and if Fisher's model is to be accepted, the Lebu were passing through the "mixing" stage. Limamou Laye was the reformer that comes to purify the "new" religion at the end of the "mixing" stage. How then, could the Layennes be syncretic in practice? They observe the five pillars of Islam, stress Islamic education, build mosques, and cling to Islamic orthodoxy. In an informal conversation with the first wife of a prominent Mouride marabout, she describes the Layennes as the "real Muslims." This opinion was repeated in many conversations with non-Layenne Senegalese Muslims. Laborde's label of syncretism is ludicrous at best.

Seeing that the Layennes had passed through previous stages of the communal "conversion" process, we must now examine why many turned to Limamou Laye. First of all we cannot ignore the overwhelmingly advanced step that Limamou Laye took when declaring the traditional castes anathema to Islamic belief. He did not just talk the talk, he walked the walk. He married wives from lower castes in order to illustrate the importance of equality among followers. The Wolof, and by extension the Lebu, divided their society into two main groups of free people: the *geer* and the *nyenyo.* The geer were those of pure noble free blood. The nyenyo are artisans who all had a non-Wolof origin. The three major groupings of nyenyo are the *jeff lek* literally those who eat from their actions meaning those who feed themselves from their work; the *sabb lek* literally those who eat from their spoken words; and the *nyool* sometimes called *semboul* who were courtesans hanging around the *geer* (nobles) serving food and drinks and eating for free. In modern-day Senegal, there are families who forbid their children from marrying into the nyenyo groups particularly the teugg (traditional metal workers) and geuwel (traditional oral historians and performers) castes. The teugg and geuwel castes are free people, but they did not work the land and thus were not noble. Slavery has disappeared and because of the way it disappeared, many slave families have disappeared into Islamic villages or urban areas, thus most do not have a memory of who is or is not a slave. The prohibition against marrying beneath one's caste was even more onerous during the days when Limamou Laye proclaimed his mission. Allowing Islam to invade such a fierce stronghold of traditional belief and practice was one more reason for many of his contemporaries to consider him mad, even those who proclaimed themselves Muslims.

Most Lebu were already affiliated with the Tijani Islamic order. Limamou Laye, however, offered a strict adherence to Islam as well as a nationalistic savior in his person. In interviews with present-day Layennes, most can recount exactly which one of their family members joined with Limamou Laye and approximately when, but most of them do not have a particular story explaining why the family member converted. This leaves us with a hole in our sources as to why people converted. What is apparent is that many of the present-day followers attribute the veracity of Mame Limamou's claims to his string of miracles. The miraculous feats of Mame Limamou and Seydina Issa are kept alive in songs and passed on to the next generation. We could easily draw conclusions that his miracles were not only the basis of his charisma as already stated but also the most important marketing factor.

One of my informants who was raised in the Layenne tariqa coming from both sides of his family, stated that after learning more about Islam, he still reveres Limamou Laye and Seydina Issa Rohou Laye, but he does not believe everything that was taught about them, primarily the story of Mame Limamou being the reincarnation of Mohammed. Others are not as candid, but many of the younger followers have shown an eagerness to embrace modernity and shy away from certain practices such as the marrying of girls at birth. Following the definition of conversion as one's religious identity, we cannot say these young followers are less ardent or less Layenne than their elders. They do attend the grand Layenne ceremonies such as the *Ajibou* or the celebration of the call of Limamou Laye, or they send money for the festival.

There are other young Layennes who have taken a keen interest in preserving their Layenne heritage. Most of these followers live in either Camberene or Yoff or nearby. Their commitment to the Layenne tradition is on display in their zealous attention to Sheriff Ousseynou Laye, the spokesman and nephew of the Khalifa-general of the tariqa. The young Layennes also have an association of Layenne students who are primarily responsible for the dissemination of information on Limamou Laye through the internet and through pamphlets. These young men and women also organize *dahiras* or spiritual educational groups that meet once a week and listen to the recitations of miracles attributed to Limamou Laye or one of his sons. They also sing and raise money. It is a social and religious group that often involves one religious leader coming and blessing the members with prayers or just his presence.

Thus, we can easily deduce that the basis of expansion of the tariqa lay in the continuation of the communal conversion that was initiated before the birth of Limamou Laye. As a reformer in Fisher's conversion model, Limamou Laye's primary mission was to purify Islam among the Lebu. It is in the role as reformer that we are better able to understand the extension of the tariqa. He presented nothing new to the Lebu people or the wider community. He recast his message in a different packaging that features his existence as the centerpiece. The packaging included a nationalist stance and as Laborde correctly points out, with direct links to the Lebu worldview couched in traditional cosmological conceptualization. The essential message, however, is the same. One of orthodox Islam consisting of submission to Allah through the path Muhammad outlined in the Qur'an.

When writing about the Aladura churches, Peel says that they are mistakenly labeled syncretic. The leaders of the Aladura churches interpret Christianity as through the prism of their cultural worldview. In much the same way, Layennism is an interpretation of Islam through the prism of Lebu cultural worldview. Syncretism is not a part of the Layenne theology and did not contribute to its expansion. On the contrary, Limamou Laye was the quintessential opponent to syncretism. Thus, we can clearly identify three factors of his message that are still quoted today as essential parts of Layenne belief and identity: pure Islamic practice and belief, Limamou Laye's identity as a reincarnation of Muhammad, and disdain for the traditional beliefs and practices. The three factors are the foundation for the expansion of the tariqa.

Chapter 7

The Legacy

Over the centuries, Senegalese Islam has changed tremendously. Though the Senegalese religious ideal continues to be a Sufi Islam expressed most commonly through allegiance to a sheikh belonging to one of the four major turuq (religious orders), the spread of Western education has led to a more individualistic approach to Islam. Rising numbers of Senegalese seeking Islamic higher education in Morocco, Sudan, and Egypt among other Middle Eastern countries have been a reforming agent in Senegalese Islam leading to a more orthodox expression under the turuq as well as the abandonment of Sufi Islam. This chapter will discuss these developments while analyzing the Layene's adaptation to the new socioreligious climate toward the end of the chapter.

Senegalese Islam and Islam in Senegal

At the dawn of the 20th century, very few citizens in the then French colony of Senegal were literate in either Arabic or the Latin alphabet. By midcentury, that number had grown tremendously. The end of the 20th century saw a record number of Senegalese seeking higher education both within the nation and abroad. The leaders of the four major turuq of Senegal sent many of their children to study in Arabic-speaking countries to continue their Islamic studies. Many disciples also sent their children abroad for study. Senegalese from the maraboutic families (religiously scholarly families) and the lay families also sent children to France and the United States. This increase in higher education has significantly changed the face of Islam in the country. In addition to the education was the advent of the internet that made all types of information readily available to those who could not afford to go abroad to study.

Added to the phenomenon of increased personal search for education is the global resurgence of orthodox Islam. Starting in the 1970's with the Iranian revolution, Islamists have begun to reassert themselves, usually violently. Just as the precolonial governments of Senegambia served as a check to the advance of vigorous Islam, the Cold War served as a check to the spread of Islamist expression of Islam. Islamists are here defined as those who wish for an Islamic government and society based on the Qur'an and the *sharia.*

With the support of the financially influential Wahabbis from Saudi Arabia, Islamist expression has increased worldwide among Muslim populations. The Revolution in Iran was hailed as a success, and others have tried to replicate it throughout the Muslim world. In Algeria, the Islamists seem not to give up. In Morocco, they are present. In Northern Nigeria, they have succeeded in imposing *sharia* in most of the Northern Nigerian states. In the West, the Islamists are on the rise using the decaying Western civilization as an example of what sin and excess can do. The universities in Senegal are teeming with hajab-sporting (head-covering) young *Ibadou* (religious) women who are Islamists.

In the wake of the attacks on the United States on 11 September 2001, many Islamists, though ardent in their belief and practice, sought to distance themselves from the more extreme and violent elements of their coreligionists in the Middle East, Afghanistan, and Pakistan. However, when the United States reacted with the invasion of Afghanistan and the preemptory strike on Iraq and subsequent regime change, the global unity of Islam caused many of the moderate and even secular Muslims to raise their voices in protest. In describing this phenomenon, Leonard Villalon seeks to make sense of the various Muslim groups crossing the "lines" of separation in order to raise a unified cry against the actions of the United States.[1] Villalon and many other scholars make a mistake in analyzing this phenomenon because of their casual attitude toward the unity of Islam. All Muslims learn to pray the same way at the same times in the same direction. If they are from a family of Muslims, some, if not all, of the posturing of Islamists were attitudes held by family members usually grandparents or parents. Thus, their love and respect for their older family members reflect adoration for their wisdom even if the younger person does not always agree. For the sake of grandma and grandpa, the practicing Muslim is in support of at least some of the Islamist positions.

In light of this situation, it is not in the least bit surprising that there was some crossing of lines among Muslims. At the end of the day with many, it is still the old Muslim against the Crusaders (*harb al-saib*) mentality when it comes to the West meddling in the affairs close to or of the Islamic holy land. After all, Osama bin Laden had no quarrel with the United States until American troops were stationed on Saudi soil. He was not the only Muslim appalled by the sight of "infidels" in the land of the two mosques. Though Islam is not a monolith, there is a core of unity usually ignored by academics in their categorization of Muslims. Categories facilitate analyses but usually ignore the more complicated similarities and differences. It is beyond the scope of our study to analyze the study of Muslim categories, yet it is an important issue which should be addressed in the social sciences.

The global restlessness among Muslims affects every country where Muslims live. Accordingly, Muslims in Senegal are experiencing a changing society and trying to find a place for their beliefs in the modern world. In Senegal this situation has, as Villalon points out, affected all the sufituruq. What Villalon fails to acknowledge is the fact that the Islamist impulse was always among the sufi turuq of Senegal no matter how seemingly latent. The Layenne strict adherence to the most extreme rules of Islam in Yoff and Camberene are clear examples.

With the Westernization (often misunderstood as modernization) of Senegalese society, the craving for a religion that the adherent can feel has not lessened. The marabout of the various turuq offer less esoteric knowledge and spiritual potency than their grandfathers and great grandfathers, but they have become effective and efficient politicians and/or businessmen. The acquisition of wealth with or without disciples has become the major focus of many men from the maraboutic families. A better educated constituency has forced many marabouts to curb some of their excesses or at least be more discreet. The resurgence of orthodox Islam has forced many marabouts to orient their message to that leaning and they at least sound more like their grandfathers and great-grandfathers. Yet, many of the intellectual elite (both secular and Islamic) are distancing themselves from the whole maraboutic enterprise. Others are working with the marabout to "tweak" their image and message.

One popular marabout is Sheikh MbayeBeychoChuchoon (beycho is the Wolof word for the traditional lingerie), a Mouride marabout who is not of the Mbacke family. He is the last of such to be made "sheikh." He has a rock star status. When he's in the arena, the crowd goes mad. His taalibes are noted for their financial success, and his daairahs are active in some of the most remote villages. One prayer from him is said to guarantee economic success. The feelings for him are so strong it destroyed a marriage. One of Sheikh Beycho's devotees refused to squash her devotion to her sheikh even when her husband, who is a rich *modoumodou,*[2] insisted. The couple divorced and Sheikh Beycho found her a richer *modoumodou* husband.[3]

Sheikh Beycho has many wives himself. More than the 4 prescribed by Islamic rules and tradition. He has openly stated that he loves women and whenever he sees a beautiful one who is single, he will marry her. He has also commented openly on his sexual prowess. Young peasant men love this exhibition of traditional machismo and hold him as an example of masculinity and spiritual sanctity even though he doesn't fit the traditional marabout mold. His sermons usually have little to do with Qur'anic exegesis or moral exhortations. Instead he flaunts his riches and personal charisma to an adoring crowd. The potency of his prayers is attested to by his many taalibes and to this even many of his detractors concede.[4]

During the 2007 Presidential Campaign in Senegal, President Abdoulaye Wade, who is an unapologetic Mouride disciple, campaigned with Sheikh Beycho. As they rode down the street in a convertible, the crowd went wild. Once they arrived at an arena a large crowd looked on in awe and adoration as Sheikh Beycho did a dance step to the music of the guewels. With the aura of a televangelist and the appeal of a rock star, Sheikh Beycho has bewitched the youth of Senegal much to the dismay of the more traditional marabout.[5]

Another example of the modernized changing marabout is the late Sheikh Imam Hassan Cisse. Sheikh Hassan completed the traditional

Islamic education in Senegal and Mauritania. He later went on to Egypt and received a B.A. degree in Islamic Sciences and Arabic Literature, an M.A. in English from University of London, and was near finishing his PhD. in Islamic studies at Northwestern University when his father died and he had to return to Kaolack to become the leader of the Niassen branch of the Tijani tariqa founded by his great-grandfather El-Hajj Abdoulaye Niasse based in Kaolack Senegal.[6]

Sheikh Hassan Cisse spoke English, French, Arabic, Hausa, and Wolof fluently. He traveled the world proselytizing and advancing the cause of many humanitarian issues. In 1988, he founded the African–American Islamic Institute, which is an NGO that operates a Qur'anic school as well as other projects for women and children. It also deals with issues such as the promotion of universal education. In 2003, he also founded Universite El-Hadji Ibrahim Niasse, which includes a medical school in Dakar, named after his grandfather.[7]

Sheikh Hassan Cisse is recognized by the international Tijani and broader Islamic community as a consummate scholar and leader. As an intellectual marabout, Sheikh Hassan Cisse represents the traditional marabout endowed with erudition and spiritual potency in addition to the occidental-savvy international leader and spokesman. His appeal is to the elite and bourgeoisie of Senegal as well as the peasants who have an attachment to the Tijanitariqa. Sheikh Hassan Cisse's most celebrated success was with the proselytization of many African Americans and Caribbean citizens.

Between the two extremes of the modern Senegalese marabout are many who tend to fall between. One such is Serin Ahkma Mbacke who has a house in Gossas, Senegal. He did his university studies in Morocco and speaks French, Arabic, as well as Wolof. His children also have command of the Arabic language. Yet he retains the appeal to the masses that many of his less educated colleagues have.

The three examples of marabout are representative of the emerging Senegalese population. There has always been a significant number of erudite marabouts in the Senegambia area, but the increase in number has been a result of globalization and the facility of international travel. As mentioned above, however, globalization has also created the paradigmatic shift whereby Muslims and non-Westerners the world over must adapt and create new means of survival amid this changing environment. The same old answers won't do for the new questions. Newly educated marabouts are offering alternative answers.

Islam and Political Legitimacy

In Senegal, the true leaders are the marabouts. An example of the potency of the marabouts is clear in a situation dealing with the taalibes. These are young boys whose families give them to the care of marabouts so that they can learn the Quran. While learning they are to beg for their food. This custom was thought to teach the boys humility and patience. There are also severe beatings for the smallest infractions. Over the years, as many marabouts have moved their operations from the rural areas where the students worked fields to the urban areas where the boys work the streets begging for food and money, the plight of the taalibes has come to the attention of visiting Westerners. Their visibly malnourished, disease-ridden, raggedly clad forms can be seen on almost any public street in Dakar and at all the bus and taxi stations. Human Rights activists and organizations have become involved in the last few decades. Yet, they approach the situation with apprehension and tact because no one wants to offend the powerful maraboutic caste.[8]

Most analysts realize the powers of the marabouts, but do not offer an explanation. The present secular government was born of the colonial government. Most Senegalese regarded the colonial conquerors as illegitimate rulers. When discussing, legitimacy, Ian Hurd invites the reader to consider "three generic reasons why an actor would obey a rule: (1) because the actor fears the punishment of rule enforcers; (2) because the actor sees the rule as in its own self interest, and (3) because the actor sees the rule as legitimate and ought to be obeyed."[9] The first instance is coercion, the second one is self-interest, and the third is legitimacy in Hurd's language.

The response of the people of present-day Senegal was to do the least of what was required of them and to continue their lives as before as much as possible. Thus, they vacillated between instances of coercion and self-interest. The attitude is the same toward the present-day Senegalese government, particularly with the present disappointment with the *sopi* of Abdoulaye Wade. *Sopi* is change in Wolof. Abdoulaye Wade and his *Partie democratique socialiste* (Democratic Socialist Party, popularly known as PDS) defeated President Abdou Diouf of the *Partie Socialiste* (Socialist Party, popularly known as PS) in the election of 2000 after more than thirty years as the opposition. In the next legislative elections, PDS won control of the *assembly nationale*. Wade moved quickly to write a new constitution which gave him unprecedented power and limited that of the other branches of government. The legislative branch has shown itself to be only a rubberstamp of Wade's wishes. Presently he rules by decree based primarily on his whim. Though he was surprised when he attempted to change the constitution in order to create a new post of vice-president (which most suspect he was going to give to his son) and reduce the required percentage of votes needed to win an election from 50% to 25%. Enraged youth protested in front of the national legislature and clashed with the riot police. Wade quickly backed down, but his mind is still turning in an attempt to try and win the election in 2012.

The young people who had such high hopes for change in 2000 have mostly resigned their hope to more of the same bad governance and ignoring of democratic institutions. Thus in times of need, the Senegalese turn to the religious leaders for guidance and/or assistance. The urban dwellers are increasingly secular in lifestyle and outlook, but their conservatively religious and cultural underpinnings rise to the top in times of adversity because they (like their ancestors) base their identity not on an individual existence, but on their existence as a part of the group, the family first and then the larger community. The family and/or community is religious and Muslim and so is the individual. The group regards the government as an illegitimate though necessary evil, so the individual adjusts his opinion to fit. The secular intellectuals even turn to the traditional leaders at points of mutual interest.

Just as Americans have created civil society groups such as labor unions, social and political associations, and other groups as a buffer between the individual and the excesses of government, the maraboutic institutions have always served as a buffer between the government and the faithful. This situation existed in the precolonial governments. The devout Muslims and their leaders acting under the state of *taqiyyah*[10] regarded the precolonial state also as a necessary evil and illegitimate institution. The problem became more acute during the colonial period notably for two reasons. Those who had served the precolonial governments entered the Islamic camp as vanquished lost sheep seeking legitimate authority. The other reason was religious. At least the precolonial monarchs were Muslim on the surface. The French made no such pretensions. They were not even a Christian government. They were strictly secular.

With the introduction of the postcolonial "independent" governments, the status of illegitimacy was not one held only by devout Muslims. Almost everyone was a devout Muslim having submitted to a sheikh. With a new dynamic, the new government is still regarded in much the same manner as the colonial government was. Many observers make much ado about the election of the Catholic Senghor as first president over the Muslim Senegalese. They simply have failed to observe over the *longue duree* in order to see the relationship between the people and their government. As representative of a government that was born of an illegitimate conquest and government, Senghor and his Muslim helpers worked with the marabouts as the French had done. In short, the people of Senegal, particularly the Muslims of Senegal, still feel and behave as a people under occupation. Of course, just as during the precolonial days, many Muslim leaders have benefitted from the status quo and do not wish to see a change. Yet the idea that the situation of *taqiyyah* would eventually die is still prominent among many, thus the door for the rise of Islamism.

Will Islamists win in Senegal? The answer is a resounding no. The day for the triumph failed with the defeat of the 17th century jihadists. The governments of Mali and Guinea-Conakry, both neighbors of Senegal, adhere closer to Islam than Senegal does. There is no room for the "mullahs" in Senegal. The conservatism of sharia is horrific to the average Senegalese. Though they agree technically with the theological premise, most would not stop their business activities half a day on Friday and five times every day during prayer. Most Senegalese would have a problem not being able to check into a hotel with a person of the opposite sex without proof of marriage. Again the average Senegalese wouldn't abandon their almost worshipful devotion to their sheikhs or the night dances of the Baye Fall just to satisfy a strict conservative interpretation of Islam. Will the elements of Islamism ever disappear in Senegal? The answer is again no and for many of the same reasons. What was supposed to be a temporary situation of enclavement, to use Lamin Sanneh's term, has become the permanent situation in Senegal. Thus, some would consider Islam in Senegal in a state of arrested development, but that observation is also incorrect. Islam in Senegal took a different path, because the progress of reformed Islam did not take off in Jolof, and the progress it made in Fouta Toro was cut short by the French conquest. The successful jihads of present-day Northern Nigeria, Mali, Guinea-Conakry, and Gambia put Islam on a different track in these respective countries. In Senegal the peaceful, though ongoing, negotiations between Islam and the secular government over time has led to another path.

Layennes and Islam

The existence of a tariqa like the Layennes is evidence of the different possibilities for Islam in Senegal. Though the Layennes have consistently preached and pushed the practices of orthodox Islam from their beginning, their assertion that Limamou Laye is the reincarnation of Muhammad limits their potential influence with other Muslims outside of Senegal. However, the brand of Islam practiced among the Layennes is as close to what the Islamist desire as one can get in the Dakar area. Over the years as the leaders of other turuq sent their children (mainly sons) to study in the Arabic world, so did the Layenne leaders. These young men were also in touch with other Muslims and exposed to various ideas. They returned with a stronger resolve toward their religious doctrine and their tariqa.

The community of Layennes experienced the same changes that the wider Senegalese populace had. It was even more acute, because most Layennes live in and around Dakar. The influences of globalization were at their door before it reached the interior. The internet cafes sprung up around them before they got to Kaolack and Tambacounda. Many of them travelled outside of Senegal before the inland population did. There was thus an urban hip aura that encompassed many of the Layennes early-on just because of their location.

How did the Layenne adapt to the rapidly changing global situation? The answer to this question seems to lie mainly in the person of the late Sheriff Ousseynou Laye. As mentioned in a previous chapter, Sheriff Ousseynou Laye was educated in France and holds a master's degree. He lived for years in the United States and is rumored to be the one who converted Michael Jackson to Islam. During the 80's, he held the same level of popularity status that Sheikh Beycho has but on a smaller scale. Over the years, his popularity has not waned, but the fervency of it all seems to have somewhat abated. His weekly meetings in the front yard of his compound were still well attended up until his untimely death. Many came to him for prayers of healing and other help. The young men who founded and hold together the student association of Layennes do so with his encouragement and support. While doing field work, I saw the activity of the young buzzing around him. He was still widely regarded as the hope for the future of the Layennetariqa.

Concrete activities that he and his group of young eager workers participate in include the development of the website and also the worldwide webcast of the *Ajibou*, which is the annual celebration of Seydina Limamou Laye's call to the service of Allah. The website has also published (in English and French) selected sermons of Limamou Laye and Seydina Issa Rohou Laye. There are circles of Layennes in North America and Europe started by Senegalese migrants but whose numbers have also been nourished by natives of North America and Europe. The information on exact numbers is not available. The majority of the members in these cells remain Senegalese migrants. Sheriff Ousseynou Laye travels often to the United States and speaks to the disciples there. He speaks English as well as French and Wolof and is thereby able to speak directly to potential disciples. In light of his education, he is also able to relate to Westerners as well as to his Senegalese congregation.

The question of growth of the tariqa is one that is pretty simple. The tariqa's potential expansion is limited due to the nature of the founder's message. It was initially explicit to the Lebu and then expanded to the wider Senegalese community and now the message has been tweaked to appeal to the mass of Blacks the world over. The obscure nature of the founder's origins and the encapsulation of the message within the confines of Islam are also limiting factors. Potential converts who are already Muslims have a problem with the assertion of Limamou Laye's person being the reincarnation of Muhammad. Potential converts who are not Muslims, have to get over the ideological hump of Islam. The concept that Muhammad is the "last" prophet is a bit much for many to swallow. The finality of it all begs the question "has God stopped speaking to mankind?" The Layennes would answer the question "no." Then there is the theological cognitive dissonance that would not sit well with a new convert to Islam. People can usually deal with cognitive dissonance theologically if they are adapting a religion to fit their own personal desires or actions. However, when a new religion is presented with the cognitive dissonance built in, it becomes a problem.

Can we then properly conjecture on the future of the Layenne tariqa? It is clear that the Layennes will not die out. They are still marrying and having children, raising them within the faith even when they move outside of Senegal. The Muride tariqa is expanding to non-Senegalese. The other turuq are not native to Senegal so their expansion has predated the creation of the state of Senegal and continues. The narrowness of the Layenne mission however continues to limit its potential dimensional growth. The more devout of the Layennes with whom I spoke seem to think that once the world hears the message of Limamou Laye, people will rush into the fold. One even encouraged me to publish this work in 2009 in order to fulfill the prophecy of Limamou Laye, which proclaims that within 100 years the whole world will have heard of his life and mission.

Conclusion

Mahdism, Sufism, and Lebu Nationalism converged upon the Western most corner of Africa in the mid-19th century. The result was Limamou Laye and the Layenne Tariqa. The tariqa and its founder responded to the expectations of the masses for the appearance of the rightly guided Mahdi. Limamou Laye also preserved his Lebu identity against Arab chauvinism by stripping Islam of Arab chauvinism and dispossessing his member followers of the idea that Arab Islam is automatically better Islam. Since Allah belongs to the world and his prophet Muhammad belongs to the world, Limamou Laye combined that idea with the concept that the Lebu were also deserving of enough attention from Allah to have their own prophet. As Muhammad is considered the last prophet, Muhammad appeared again just for the Lebu and all blacks by extension.

The introduction of Islam to the Senegambia (using Boubacar Barry's definition, it is an area encompassing present day Southern Mauritania, Senegal, Gambia, and Guinea as well as Southwestern Mali) was a gradual and mostly peaceful process. The expansion of the faith, however, took on two extremes: violent jihad and peaceful penetration. The peaceful penetration was usually followed by a wave of violent jihad as the number of Muslims grew strong enough to envision a victory. This pattern was repeated all over the region with various adjustments and results. In Senegal, the jihadists saw their efforts running into the colonial conquest. The French colonial government helped the precolonial governments defeat the jihadists and then used that intervention as an entry point to destroy the authority of the precolonial governments' sovereignty. The Muslims who survived the jihads took advantage of the colonial conquest to welcome into their number the defeated soldiers and noble families. Into such an environment, Limamou Laye launched his call for followers.

Though Islam had followed a slightly different path on the Cap-Verde where Libasse Chaw/Limamou Laye was born and raised, the same essential process of penetration and reform was in progress. The creation of a theocratic republic in the late 18th century among the Lebu contributed to a strengthening of the Islam already present but also left room for syncretism. Limamou Laye challenged the existing order while introducing new development to the eschatological doctrine of Mahdism.

The concept of the Mahdi has a long history among Muslims and, as it spreads mainly orally, has taken various forms throughout the Muslim world with many Christian eschatological influences as well as Judaic and other pre-Islamic religious borrowings. While examining the mission of Limamou and the consequential tariqa, it is clear that his mission borrowed from the traditional beliefs and practices that his people have followed for centuries before and after the introduction of Islam. His theological feature of reincarnation has a clear link to the pre-Islamic Lebu beliefs. His concentration on healing was the central mandate of the pre-Islamic religion. In the pre-Islamic religion, a proper relationship had to be maintained between the physical and the spiritual world. If those in the physical world committed an infraction, reprisals would be forthcoming from the spiritual world. The role of the priests was to maintain a working pleasant relationship with the spirit world. This included appeasement in order to cure diseases as all diseases were the result of some spiritual infraction. Limamou Laye's appearance and mission was set to reestablish the link between the Lebu community and God. The Lebu had turned against God through their lax Islamic practices and their mixing of religions.

Limamou Laye also brought the Lebu into the global arena through his insistence on an internationally recognized religion and the God of that religion speaking specifically to a small group in Cap-Vert. This process was repeated throughout Africa and Asia as global trade and later colonization made smaller isolated societies aware of the rest of the world forcing these societies to define their place in it or have their placed defined for them. This development should not be underestimated. Limamou's proclamation, however, did more because it made Muhammad specifically for the Lebu. So he brought Islam to the Lebu on Lebu terms in the Lebu language.

The whole goal of religion is to make sense of man's place in the world in relation to his natural and spiritual environment. Once the natural environment includes more stimuli than in previous generations, the local cosmology and theology has to be revamped or at least tweaked in order to take into account the novelties. The Lebu had been in contact with Europeans, Arabs, and other sub-Saharan Africans for approximately four centuries. Islam had been among them for at least that long, many of them having brought it with them as they migrated from the interior. The fleeing marabouts under Jaal Joop institutionalized Islam in the area when organizing the government. Limamou Laye raised Islam to another level as a reformer following the pattern that had been playing out for centuries in other parts of the continent and Senegambia particularly. In doing so, he tightened the belt between the Lebu Islamic practices and orthodox Islam as prescribed by the Arab world and interpreted by Limamou Laye. Seydina Issa Rohou Laye further tightened it by bringing the internationally recognized eschatological Islamic doctrinal drama into a local sphere proclaiming himself the reincarnation of Issa ibn Mariama (Jesus Christ).

Being illiterate and knowing just enough Arabic to pray, Limamou Laye rendered his sermons in Wolof and they all reinforced the moral standards and other rules found in the Qur'an and the Hadith. Thus again he managed to localize the global through his delivery. His traditional esoteric knowledge and ability combined with his insistence on orthodox Islam to bring a new voice and interpretation to Sufi Islam. In other words, Limamou Laye's localization of the global fits into the ongoing negotiation between the traditional societies and Islam, fitting into the larger conversation between the localized and the global.

The point of our study, however, has been to show that Limamou Laye al-Mahdiyyou was an African Islamic creation and not a result of French colonization as Cecile Laborde asserts.[1] The rise of claims of Mahdism throughout the Muslim world was not the result of colonization as many scholars have assumed. The oral tradition of the

Mahdi describes him appearing at a time when Islam is threatened. There was expectancy for him to come at the beginning of the 12th century of the hegira, which happens to coincide with the 19th century of the Gregorian calendar being the century of the start of European conquest and colonization. The whole Islamic thrust occurring in the 19th century was a globalizing influence predating European contact while running parallel to European trade/colonization. The one did not cause the other, though they did develop a symbiotic relationship as colonization obliterated Islam's major obstacle to expansion, the precolonial sociopolitical order.

In the case of Limamou Laye, the precolonial sociopolitical order was not initially an obstacle. As his prestige and standing grew, however, they felt their authority threatened and actually worked with the French in order to undermine Limamou Laye's movement. The same thing happened to Sheikh Ahmadou Bamba Mbacke as well as other religious leaders. Limamou Laye's hagiographers portray how all his enemies, Lebu and French, were punished for their part in his deportation. Whether it was divine punishment or not is debatable. What is sure is Limamou Laye's tariqa has outlasted his detractors, giving his followers an opportunity to flourish.

Notes

Introductions

[1] Nehemia Levtzion. "Patterns of Islamization in West Africa" found in *Islam in West Africa*. (Brookfield, Vermont: Variorum, 1994), p. 1–208.
[2] Lamine Sanneh "The Domestication of Islam and Christianity in African Societies: A Methodological Approach" *Journal of Religion in Africa* Vol. 11, fasc 3. 1980 p. 3.
[3] Sanneh, Domestication. p. 1.
[4] David Robinson. *The Holy War of Umar Tal: The Western Sudan in the mid-19th Century*. New York: Oxford University Press, 1985; Donal Cruise O'Brien. *The Mourides of Senegal. The Political and Economic Organization of an Islamic Brotherhood.* Oxford: Claredon Press, 1971; Paul Marty *Etudes sur l'Islam au Senegal.* Paris: E. Leroux, 1917; J. Spencer Trimingham, *Islam in West Africa.* Oxford: Claredon Press, 1959.
[5] Mamadou Diouf *Le Kajoor au XIX Siecle: pouvoir ceddo et conquete coloniale.* Paris: Karthala, 1990; Boubacar Barry *Le royaume de Waalo: le Senegal avant la conquete.* Paris: Karthala, 1985; Barry *Senegambia and the Atlantic Slave Trade.* Cambridge: Cambridge University Press, 1998.
[6] Lamin Sanneh *The Jakhanke: the history of an Islamic Clerical Peoples of the Senegambia.* London: International African Institute, 1979.

Chapter 1

[1] Qur'an 2:129–31; 5:41–51;42:13–18; 61:6; 80:11.
[2] Martin Lings. *Muhammad: His life based on the earliest sources.* Cambridge, UK: Islamic Texts Society, 1995, passim.
[3] Karen Armstrong, *Islam: a short history.* New York: Random House, 2002, p. 33.
[4] Gordon Darnell Newby, *The Making of the Last Prophet: A reconstruction of the earliest biography of Muhammad.* Columbia, SC: University of South Carolina Press, 1989, passim.
[5] Ibid, 4.
[6] Annemarie Schimmel. *Mystical Dimensions of Islam.* Chapel Hill, NC: UNC Press, 1975, p. 214.
[7] Ibid, 216; Sura 21 verse 107.
[8] Qur'an 6:101; 37:149–53; 19:17–27.

[9] Qur'an 4:157–8.
[10] Qur'an Surah 56.
[11] M. Mushin Khan, Translation of *Sahih Bukhari.* http://www.iium.edu.my/deed/hadith/bukhari/index.html

Chapter 2

[1] Peter Clarke. *West Africa and Islam: A study of religious development from the 8th to the 20th century.* London: Edward Arnold, Ltd, 1982, pp. 8–9.
[2] The Kharijites broke away from the Shi a Ali, or partisans of Ali, when Ali sought to compromise with Muwiya over the succession dispute following the death of Uthman in 656. It was a Kharijite who killed Ali in 661. One of the main arguments of the Kharijite was that the leaders should be chosen by a group of holy men and not by primogeniture based on the Quraysh tribe. The Ibadite branch of the Kharijites is a group of followers of Abu Allah ibn Ibad from Basra, Iraq. His followers established colonies in North Africa and are numerous in Oman. They are a fundamentalist group who frown upon moderate Muslims and non-Muslims, but unlike their Kharijite forbearers, they do not consider moderate Muslims *kaffir.*
[3] ElHadji Rasane Mbaye *Islam au Senegal* unpublished doctoral dissertation Universite Cheikh Anta Diop Dakar 1975–6, p. 59.
[4] Humphrey J. Fisher. "What's in a name? The Almoravids of the Eleventh Century in the Western Sahara" *Journal of Religion in Africa* vol. 22, no. 4 (1992) p. 290; H. T. Norris. "New Evidence on Abdullah Yasin and the Origins of the Almoravids." *Journal of African History.* Vol. 12, no. 2 (1971): pp. 255–7.
[5] Clarke, *West Africa and Islam,* pp. 17–20.; Mervyn Hiskett *The Course of Islam in Africa.* Edinburgh: Edinburgh University Press, 1994. p. 93.
[6] Nehemia Levtzion and J. F. P Hopkins eds., Hopkins trans. *Corpus of Early Arabic Sources for West African History,* (Cambridge: Cambridge University Press, 1981), p. 82.
[7] Cheikh Anta Babou *Fighting the Greater Jihad: Ahmadu Bamba and the founding of the Muridiyya of Senegal, 1853–1913.* (Athens, Ohio: The University of Ohio Press, 2007), p. 22.
[8] Corpus, p. 268.
[9] Lamine Sanneh *The Jakhanke.*
[10] David Wilkinson "Spatio-Temporal Boundaries of African Civilizations Reconsidered" Presented to the 22nd Annual Meeting of the International Society for the Comparative Study of Civilizations, Scranton, Pennsylvania, June 3–6, 1993 (not paginated).
[11] Lamine Sanneh. "Futa Jallon and the Jakhanke Traditon, Part I: The Historical Setting." *Journal of African History* 12:1 (1981), p. 42.
[12] Mbaye, pp. 59–61.
[13] David Robinson. *Muslim Societies in African History,* (New York: Cambridge University Press, 2004). p. 27.

[14] Diouf *Le Kajoor* pp. 83–95.

[15] Ibid., Eunice Charles "Shaikh Amadu Ba and Jihad in Jolof" *International Journal of African Historical Studies* vol. 8, no. 3, p. 270.

[16] Pierre Labat *Afrique Occidentale* quoted in Gwendolyn Midlo Hall *Africans in Colonial Louisiana: The Development of Afro-Creole Culture in the Eighteenth Century.* (Baton Rouge, Louisiana: Louisiana State University Press, 1992), p. 38.

[17] Douglas Streusand, "What Does Jihad Mean?", *Middle East Quarterly.* September 1997, p.3.

[18] Phillip Curtin "Jihad in West Africa: Early Phases and Inter-Relations between Senegal and Mauritania." *The Journal of African History.* 12:1 (1971), p. 14.

[19] Ibid pp. 15–16.

[20] Ibid. pp. 19–22; Clarke, *West Africa and Islam,* pp. 83–6.

[21] Michael Gomez *Pragmatism in the Age of Jihad: The Pre-Colonial State of Bundu.* Cambridge: Cambridge University Press, 1992; Clark, Andrew. "The Fulbe of Bundu (Senegambia): From Theocracy to Secularization." *The International Journal of African Historical Studies,* Vol. 29, No. 1. (1996), pp. 1–23.

[22] Diouf, pp. 90–1, pp. 96–8.

[23] Cheikh Anta Diop, *Pre-colonial Black Africa,* Brooklyn, NY: Lawrence Hill Books, pp. 71–2; Assane Sylla in intro. to Mbaye Thiam, *Entretien sur l'histoire des lebous de La Pres'Ile du Cap-Vert* unpublished, Archives d'Institute Fondementale d'Afrique Noire, Universite Cheikh Anta Diop Dakar, 1970, pp. 1–4.

[24] Basil Davidson, *Africa in History.* New York: Touchstone, 1995, pp. 252–4.

[25] Archives National de France (Section outré-mer), S and D 1 dossier 54, November 27, 1867. Quoted in Diouf, p. 238.

[26] Andrew F. Clark "The Fulbe of Bondu" pp. 1–23; Humphrey Fisher "The Early Life of Al-Hajj Muhammad Al-Amin the Soninke" *The Journal of African History* Vol. 11, No. 1 (1970), pp. 51–69.

[27] Khadim Mbacke *Sufism and Religious Brotherhoods in Senegal.* Trans. Eric Ross. Markus Weiner Publishers: Princeton, NJ, 2005, pp. 42–3.

[28] Amar Samb, *Essai sur la contribution du Senegal à la literature d'expression arabe* (Dakar: IFAN, 1972), p. 428.

[29] David Shank, "The Taming of the Prophet Harris" *The Journal of Religion in Africa.* Vol. 27, Fasc 1. (Feb. 1997), p. 64.

[30] Lamine Sanneh, *Disciples of all Nations: Pillars of World Christianity.* (Oxford: Oxford University Press, 2008), p. 174.

[31] Jamil M. Abun-Nasr *Muslim Communities of Grace: The Sufi Brother hoods in Islamic Religious Life.* (New York: Columbia University Press, 2007).

[32] Ibid., 15, pp. 24–6.

[33] Wolof word for foreigner.

[34] Amar Samb, *Essai sur la . . .,* p. 428.

[35] Serigne Bachir Mbacké, *Les bienfaits de l'éternel, ou, La biographie de Cheikh Ahmadou Bamba Mbacké* (traduction par Khadim Mbacké), Dakar, IFAN/ Cheikh Anta Diop, 1995, p. 339.

[36] Ibid., p. 350

[37] In Wolof society, this is what a slave does when a new master buys him.

Chapter 3

[1] Mamadou Diouf, *Le Kajoor au XIVeme siècle.* Karthala, 1991, pp. 23–5.

[2] G. Balandier and P. Mercier, *Les pecheurs Lebou du Senegal: particularisme et evolution.* (St. Louis, Senegal: Centre d'IFAN, 1952), pp. 211–12.; Richard Dumez and Moustapha Ka *Yoff le territoire assiégé: Un village lébou dans la banlieue de Dakar.* (Paris: l'organisation des nations unies pour l'education, la science, et la culture, 2000), p. 13.

[3] Assane Sylla, *Le peuple lebou de la presqu'ile du Cap-Vert.* (Dakar: Les nouvelles Editions Africaines du Senegal, 1992), p. 11.

[4] Dumez, p. 13.

[5] Sylla, pp. 11–14.

[6] Dumez, pp. 14–17.

[7] Thiam *Entretien sur l'histoire des lebous de La Pres'Ile du Cap-Vert,* 1970, p. 6.

[8] Diop *Pre-colonial Black Africa,* pp. 69–72.

[9] Sylla gives 1790 as the year of independence. G. T. Mollien, the French explorer who was in Cayor at the time, gives 1798 as the year of the battle. I chose 1798 because Jaal Joop was instrumental in establishing the independent government and he did not come to the Lebu until 1795.

[10] Diouf, pp. 98–102, Sylla pp. 14–18.

[11] Sylla, pp. 17–27.; Dumez, p. 16.

[12] Diop, pp. 70–2.

[13] A. Zempleni "La dimension therapeutique du culte des rab Ndep Tuuru et Samp: Rites de possession chez les lebou et les wolofs" *Psychopathologie Africaine* Vol III, no. 3 Dakar 1966, p. 302.

[14] Cecile Laborde *La Confriererie Layenne et les Lebou du Senegal: Islam et culture tradionnelle en Afrique.* (Bordeaux: CEAN, 1995), p. 31.

[15] G. J. Duchemin « La Republique Lebou et le peuplement actuel de La Presqu'Ile du Cap-Vert » *Etudes Senegalaises* (Dakar: IFAN, 1949), pp. 297–9.

[16] Ibid.

[17] Zempleni, pp. 305–7.

[18] Modesty is a large part of Wolof politeness. Thus, people usually do not brag about their acquisitions particularly when they are servants of the people.

[19] Zempleni, p. 307.

[20] Ibid.

[21] Assane Sylla, *Les Prophetes Seydina Limamou Le Mahdi et Seydina Issa Rouhou Lahi* (Dakar, Senegal: Imprimerie Saint-Paul, 1989), p. 8.

[22] Diop, pp. 71–2, Assane Sylla in intro. to Thiam, pp. 1–4.

[23] Diouf, p. 101.

[24] Surat Al-Hijr 15:26–7; Surat Al-Jinn 72: 1–2

[25] Dumez, pp. 42–3; During my conversations with Senegalese Muslims, the conversion of jinn to Islam was mentioned many times.

[26] Sylla, 53.

[27] Edward Said *Orientalism* (New York: Pantheon, 1978), pp. 1–28.

[28] Emmanuel Eze, ed. *Race and the Enlightenment: A Reader* (Oxford: Blackwell Publishers, 2001), von Herder pp. 71–8, Kant p. 57.

[29] William Cohen *The French Encounter with Africans: White Responses to Blacks, 1530–1880* (Bloomington, Indiana: University of Indiana Press, 2003), 1.
[30] Ibid, pp. 3–6, 9–19.
[31] Ibid.,
[32] Memmi, p. 121.
[33] Ibid.
[34] Christopher Harrison *France and Islam in West Africa, 1860–1960.* (Cambridge: Cambridge University Press, 1988); David Robinson. *Paths to Accommodation: Muslim Societies and French Colonial Authorities in Senegal and Mauritania, 1880–1920.* (Athens, Ohio: Ohio State University Press, 2000).
[35] Alioune Diop, "Niam n'goura: ou les raisons d'etre de *Presence Africaine*" quoted in James Genova. *Colonial Ambivalence, Cultural Authenticity, and the Limitations of Mimicry in French-Ruled West Africa, 1914–1956.* (New York: Peter Lang Publishing, Inc, 2004), p. 1.

Chapter 4

[1] Charles, "Jihad in Jolof . . ." 371.
[2] http://www.layene.sn/l_francais/limamou.php
[3] Recounted in an interview on January 31, 2008 with Serigne Mbacké Laye, official spokesperson for the Khalifa General of the Layenne tariqa, Camberene, Senegal.
[4] Ibid.
[5] Cheikh Moktar Lo, trans. Assane Sylla, « La vie de Seydina Mohamadou Limamou Laye » *Bulletin de l'IFAN,* y. XXXIV, série B, n° 3, juillet 1972, p. 7.
[6] General West African word for foreigner.
[7] Reference to Ali-Bakr, the assistant to the prophet Mohammed.
[8] Samb, *Essai,* p. 428.
[9] Interview with Binta Fall summer 1999.
[10] http://www.layene.sn/l_francais/limamou.php
[11] Some Muslims interpret John 15:26 as the foretelling of Muhammad's coming while most Christians believe Jesus was referring to the Holy Ghost.
[12] http://www.layene.sn/l_francais/limamou.php
[13] El Hajj Malik Sarr, *Ajibou da Iyallah ou La vie exemplaire de Limamou Laye* (Dakar: Imprimerie Nouvelle, 1966), p. 9.
[14] http://www.layene.sn/l_francais/limamou.php
[15] Sarr, *La vie exemplaire . . .,* p. 9.
[16] While living in Gossas Senegal (2005–6), I had neighbors whose twin sons were mentally ill but harmless. The whole family had mental problems emanating, according to various informants, from a curse that someone had put on their father during a land dispute. No one bothered the twins even though they would often make a lot of noise at night disturbing the whole quarter. One man who was high on drugs hit his mother, violating the sacred respect for parents, the whole community tied him down and beat him nearly to death. By the time the police came to arrest him, they actually had to rescue him from the crowd and take him in for medical attention.

[17] Boubou or booba is a general West African word for the traditional clothing.

[18] http://www.layene.sn/1_francais/limamou.php

[19] Ibid.

[20] Eunice Charles, p. 371.

[21] Rose Lake, "The Making of a Mouride Mahdi: Serigne Abdoulaye Yakhine Diop of Thies," in *African Islam and Islam in Africa: Encounters between Sufis and Islamists*. Eva E. Rosander and David Westerlund eds. (Athens, Ohio: The Ohio University Press, 1997), pp. 217–53.

[22] Clarke, *Mahdism in West Africa*, pp. 19–29.

Chapter 5

[1] William L. Cleveland, *A History of the Modern Middle East*, Boulder: Westview Press, 1994, p. 34.

[2] Karen Armstrong, *Islam: A Short History*. (New York: The Modern Library, 2002), pp. 67–9; D. Josiya Negahban, "Muhammad Al-Mahdi" in Lexilook Encyclopaedia, 1996, http://lexicorient.com/e.o/12thimam.htm

[3] John R. Willis, "Jihad fi Sabil Allah- Its Doctrinal Basis in Islam and Some Aspects of its evolution in Nineteenth Century West Africa," *The Journal of African History*, vol. 8, no. 3 (1967), p. 404.

[4] Clarke, *Mahdism in West Africa*, pp. 20–2.

[5] *Ibid.*, 19–29.

[6] Ibid.

[7] Humphrey Fisher. "The Early Life . . ." p. 60. Humphrey does not believe that Lamine ever proclaimed that he was the mahdi, but he sites French sources that make the claim.

[8] Eunice Charles "Shaikh Amadu Ba . . ." p. 270.

[9] Martin Z. Njeuma. "Adamawa and Mahdism: The Career of Hayatu Ibn Sa'id in Adamawa, 1878–1898" *Journal of African History* 12:1, 1971, p. 62.

[10] Paul Lovejoy and J.S. Hogendorn. "Revolutionary Mahdism and the Resistance to Colonial Rule, 1905–06." *Journal of African History*, vol. 31, no. 2, 1990, pp. 217–44.

[11] Muhammad Umar, "Muslims' Eschatological Discourses on Colonialism in Northern Nigeria," *Journal of the American Academy of Religion*, vol. 67, no. 1 (1999), pp. 59–84.

[12] Assane Sylla, *Les Prophetes Seydina Limamou Le Mahdi et Seydina Issa Rouhou Lahi* (Dakar, Senegal: Imprimierie Saint-Paul, 1989), pp. 15–16.

[13] Ibid.

[14] Khadim Mbacke, trans. Eric Ross, *Sufism and Religious Brotherhoods in Senegal*. (Princeton: Markus Weiner Publishers, 2005), pp. 70–1.

[15] David Robinson, *Paths of Accommodation: Muslim Societies and French Colonial Authorities in Senegal and Mauritania, 1880–1920* (Athens, Ohio: Ohio University Press, 2000), p. 5.

[16] Sylla, pp. 11–19.

[17] Lo, passim.

[18] Mark 5:10–20; Luke 4:34 *Holy Bible.*

[19] Letter dated 21 July 1890 to the l'Administrateur principal des Cercles de Dakar et Thiès, found in the Archives Nationales du Senegal.

[20] Cecile Laborde, *La Confrérie Layenne et les Lébou du Sénégal: Islam et culture traditionnelle en Afrique* (Bourdeaux: Centre d'etude d'Afrique Noire, 1995), p. 18.

[21] Diop, pp. 172–5.

[22] In a private conversation with a grandson of Cheikh Ahmadou Bamba Mbacké, I asked his family origins and he told me they came from the prophet's family.

[23] Lamine Sanneh *Disciples of All Nations: Pillars of World Christianity.* (Oxford: Oxford University Press, 2008), p. 164.

[24] Jamil M. Abun-Nasr, *Muslim Communities of Grace: The Sufi Brother hoods in Islamic Religious Life.* (New York: Columbia University Press, 2007).

[25] Mechal Sobel, *Trablin' On: The Slave Jouney to an Afro-Baptist Faith* (Westport, Conneticut: Greenwood Press, 1979); Albert Raboteau, *SlaveReligion: The "Invisible Institution" in the Antebellum South.* (New York: Oxford University Press, 1978).

[26] While the author was living in Gossas, Senegal the Baay Fall would regularly have all-night dances.

[27] Andras Zempleni « L'enfant nit ku bon: Un tableau psycho-pathologique traditionnel chez les Wolof et Lebou du Sénégal ». 1965 Psychopathologie Africaine, vol. 13, pp. 329–441.

[28] Limamou Laye "Les sermons de Seydina Limamou Laye et son fils Seydina Issa Rohou Lahi" http://www.siup.sn/ael/, 1–18; Sylla 5–10.

[29] Laye, pp. 5–6, 9–10.

[30] Sarr, pp. 12–14.

[31] Sarr, p. 19.

[32] Undated letter from Agent Mbaye to Commisaire de la police M. Milanini, found in the Archives Nationales du Senegal.

[33] Sarr, pp. 20–1; Sylla, *Soleil de l'Occident,* Dakar: self-published, p. 21.

[34] Ibid., p. 22.

[35] Sylla, *Prophets* pp. 52–3; Sarr, *Ajibou,* p. 19.

[36] Assane Sylla for Fondation Seydina Issa Rouhou Lahi Mouvement des Jeunes *La Face Cachée de L'exil de Seydina Limamou Lahi Al Mahdi à Gorée* (Dakar: M.INT./DAGAT, 1991), p. 11.

[37] "Every innovation is a misguidance and every misguidance leads to hellfire" is found in collection of hadith commonly called *Sahih Muslim* (book 6, 21) collected by Muslim ibn Hajjaj also known as Imam Muslim. *Sahih Muslim* is the second most respected collection of the "canonical" hadith.

[38] Sarr, p. 11.

[39] Ibid, p. 17. Translation from Wolof with the aide of Marie-Rose Bob.

[40] Ibid, p. 22.

Chapter 6

[1] Donal Cruise O'Brien and Christian Coulon eds. *Charisma and Brotherhood in African Islam*, (Oxford: Claredon Press, 1988).
[2] Max Weber, *Max Weber On Charisma and Institution Building*, (Chicago: University of Chicago Press, 1968), pp. 18–27.
[3] Sylla, *Les Prophets*, p. 85.
[4] Ibid.
[5] Ibid. p. 94.
[6] Ibid. pp. 101–3.
[7] These are the formal names of the Mame Limamou and Seydina Issa articulated by their Arabized followers.
[8] One of my informants had to rescue his girlfriend, who is not Layenne, from such a band in May of 2005.
[9] J. D. Y. Peel. "Syncretism and Religious Change," *Comparative Studies in Society and History*, Vol. 10, no. 2, (Jan. 1968), p. 130.
[10] Robin Horton, "On the Rationality of Conversion, Part I," *Africa* , 45 (1975), p. 219.
[11] Humphrey Fisher "Conversion Reconsidered: Some Historical Aspects of Religious Conversion in Black Africa," *Africa* 43, 1973.
[12] James Searing, "Conversion to Islam: Military Reruitment and Generaltional Conflict in a Sereer-Safen Village (Bandia), 1920–38," *Journal of African History*. Vol. 44, No.1 (2003) pp. 73–94.
[13] Quentin Gausset, "Islam or Christianity? The choices of the Wawa and the Kwanja of Cameroon," *Africa:Journal of the International African Institute*. Vol. 69. No. 2 (1999).

Chapter 7

[1] Leonard Villalon, "Senegal: Islamism on a Sufi Landscape" in *Political Islam in West Africa*, William F. S. Miles, ed. London: Lynne Reinner Publisher, 2007.
[2] Colloquial Wolof for a Senegalese who lives and works abroad. It is a comical jab at the most popular name in Senegal (and the world) Mohammad and its derivative Ahmadu or Modu. The female Senegalese expatriates are sometimes called Fatoufatou again a jab at the most popular female Senegalese name.
[3] The bride in this story is the daughter of a friend of the author.
[4] In conversation with a Mouride Marabout of the Mbacke family, he derided Serin Beycho yet conceded to his spiritual potency.
[5] The author was in Senegal at the time and witnessed this scene on television. The author has noted in the past few years the increasing numbers of young people who wear the picture of Sheikh Beycho around their necks regardless of the tariqa affiliation of their families.
[6] www.tijani.org; www.thefaydah.org
[7] www.aaii.info

[8] Donna L. Perry, "Muslim Child Disciples, Global Civil Society, and Children's Rights in Senegal: The Discourse of Strategic Structuralism," *Anthropological Quarterly* vol. 77, no 1 (Winter 2004), pp. 47–86.

[9] Ian Hurd, "Legitimacy and Authority in International Politics," *International Organization* Vol. 53, no. 2 (Spring, 1999), p. 379.

[10] It is an Islamic doctrine that allows a Muslim to be lax on certain Islamic rules and regulations or even deny being a Muslim when he/she is in the minority and/or powerless to enforce Islamic law or better his/her situation. See Chapter 2.

Conclusion

[1] Laborde, *Layenes*

Bibliography

Primary Resources

Laye, Limamou. Sermons transcribed in Arabic by Tafsir Abdou Gaye, translated into French by Assane Sylla. They are on the official website of the organization.

Lo, Cheikh Mokhtar. "La vie de Seydina Mohammadou Limamou Laye traduite et annotée par El-Hadji Mouhamadou Sakhir Gaye et Assane Sylla." *Bulletin d'IFAN* B, no. 3 (1971): pp. 497–523. (Lo, a contemporary of Limamou Laye wrote a biography in Arabic, this article is a French translation of the biography)

Marty, Paul. *Etudes sur L'Islam au Senega:*. Paris: E. Leroux, 1917.

Nehemia Levtzion, J. F. P. Hopkins. *Corpus of Early Arabic Sources for West African History*. Trans. F. P. K. Hopkins. Cambridge: Cambridge University Press, 1981.

The Qur'an: Arabic Text with Corresponding English Meanings. Riyad: Abul Qasim Publishing House, 1997.

Sylla, Assane. *Le Mahdi Seydina Limamou Lahi: Soleil de l'Occident*. Dakar, 1990. (collection of sermons and stories)

Sylla, Assane. "Les persecutions de Seydina Mohamadou Limamou Laye par les autorites coloniales," *Bulletin de l'IFAN*. B, no. 4 (1971): pp. 590–641. (collection of official correspondence and orders concerning Limamou Laye's arrest and exile with commentary)

Thiam, Mbaye. "Entretien sur l'histoire des Lebou et de la presque-ile." Trans. Assane Sylla. Dakar: Archives d'Institut Fondamental d'Afrique Noire, Universite Chiekh Anta Diop, 1970.

Archives

Archives de l'Institut Fondemental d'Afrique Noire Universite Cheikh Anta Diop de Dakar

Archives Nationale de la France, Section d'Outre mer

Archives Nationale du Senegal, Fonds Senegal Colonial, Section B Correspondence generale, 10D3/0007

Interviews

Much of my information was gathered in informal conversations, after which I would go home and write notes from memory. Senegalese, as well as most West Africans, consider knowledge to be something of great value to be hidden. Secrecy is a cultural trait, and thus outright request for interviews are often denied or the information is amended in light of the situation. Thus, in many instances, I resorted to working my topic in leisurely conversations over ataaya in the evenings with young men, after lunch over watermelon squares, in taxis with taxi-men (a Moroccan taxi-man in Paris provided a lot of information on bid'ah or innovation) and even in chat sessions on msn instant messenger. The interviews below are mostly formal. I also learned much in which to contextualize my findings just from living among the Wolof and observing.

My wife Fatou Souare is an adherent of the Layenne tariqa. She provided much help in translation and even conducted a few interviews, recording them for me. In addition, Fatou also was an informant giving her perspective as a Layenne as was her cousins Seydina Mbaye, Libasse Mbaye, and El Hajj Malik Mbaye in informal conversations.

June 10, 1999, Binta Fall.

May 2–29, 2005, Mokhtar Laye – we discussed everyday when I finished my archival work. Camberene, Senegal.

May 5, 2005, Anta Thiam Laye Cite des Enseignants, Senegal.

May 12, 2005, Anta Souare, Camberene Senegal. (she also performed songs that I recorded on my video camera)

May 12, 2005, Big Laye, Camberene Senegal. (he was also my informal tour guide at Jaamalaye, the mausoleum of Seydina Issa Rohou Laye)

February 2006, El Hajj Mbaye Dianka Gossas, Senegal.

August 6, 2006; December 28, 2007; Njaga Ka and his brother Ahmadou Ka, Gossas, Senegal.

January 28, 2008 Marietou Ndiaye, interview by Fatou Thomas, Yembeul, Senegal.

January 28, 2008 Aida Diop and her daughter Fatou Diop, interview by Fatou Thomas, Yembeul, Senegal.

January 31, 2008, Serigne Mbacke Laye , interview by Fatou Thomas. Spokesperson for the Khalifa-General of the Layenne Tariqa, Camberene, Senegal.

Mame Gueye March 17, 2009.

Ware Diene April 11, 2009.

Secondary Sources

Websites

Layenne. www.layene.sn/l_francais/limamou.php (official site of the organization)

Negahban, D. Josiya. "Muhammad al-Mahdi." *Look Lex Encyclopaedia.* 1996. http://lexicorient.com/e.o/12thimam.htm (accessed January 2009).

Unpublished Material

Mbaye, El Hadji Rasane. "Islam au Senegal." Dakar: Universite Cheikh Anta Diop, Unpublished doctoral dissertation.

Articles

Charles, Eunice. "Shaikh Amadu Ba and Jihad in Jolof." *International Journal of African Historical Studies*, 1975: pp. 367–82.

Clark, Andrew. "The Fulbe of Bundu (Senegambia): From Theocracy to Secularization." *International Journal of African Historical Studies*, 1996: pp. 1–23.

Curtin, Phillip. "Jihad in West Africa: Early Phases and Inter-Relations between Senegal and Mauritania." *Journal of African History*, 1971: pp. 11–24.

Duchemin, G. J. "La Republique Lebou et le peuplement actuel de La Presqu'Ile du Cap-Vert ." *Etudes Senegalaises*, 1949: pp. 289–304.

Fisher, Humphrey. "Conversion Reconsidered: Some Historical Aspects of Religious Conversion in Black Africa." *Africa* 43, no. 1 (1973): pp. 27–40.

Fisher, Humphrey J. "What's in a name?: the Almoravids of the 11th Century in Western Sahara." *Journal of Religion in Africa*, 1992: pp. 290–317.

Fisher, Humphrey. "The Early Life of Al-Hajj Muhammad Al-Amin the Soninke." *Journal of African History*, 1970: pp. 51–69.

Gausset, Quentin. "Islam or Christianity? The choices of teh Wawa and the Kwanja of Cameroon." *Africa: Journal of the International African Institute* 69, no. 2 (1999): pp. 257–78.

Horton, Robin. "On the Rationality of Conversion, Part I." *Africa* 45, no. 4 (1975): pp. 373–99.

Hurd, Ian. "Legitimacy and Authority in International Politics." *International Organization* 53, no. 2 (1999): pp. 379–408.

Lake, Rose. "The Making of a Mouride Mahdi: Serigne Abdoulaye Yakhine Diop of Thies." *African Islam and Islam in Africa: Encounters between Sufis and Islamists*, eds. Eva Evers Rosander and David Westerlund. Athens, Ohio: The University of Ohio Press, 1997.

Levtzion, Nehemia. "Patterns of Islamization in West Africa." *Islam in West Africa*, ed. Nehemia Levtzion, pp. 1–30. Brookfield, Vermont: Ashgate Variorum, 1994.

Lovejoy, Paul and J. S. Hogendorn. "Revolutionary Mahdism and the Resistance to Colonial Rule, 1905–06." *Journal of African History* 31, no. 2 (1990): pp. 217–44.

Njeuma, Martin Z. "Adamawa and Mahdism: The Career of Hayatu Ibn Sa'id in Adamawa, 1878-1898." *Journal of African History*, 1971: pp. 61–77.

Norris, H. T. "New Evidence on Abdullah Yasin and the Origins of the Almoravids." *Journal of African History*, 1971: pp. 255–68.

Peel, J. D. Y. "Syncretism and Religious Change." *Comparitive Studies in Society and History* 10, no. 2 (1968): pp. 121–41.

Perry, Donna L. "Muslim Child Disciples, Global Civil Society, and Children's Rights in Senegal: The Discourse of Strategic Structuralism." *Anthropological Quarterly* 77, no. 1 (2004): pp. 47–86.

Sanneh, Lamin. "Futa Jallon and the Jakhanke clerical tradition. Part I: the historical setting." *Journal of African History*, 1981: pp. 38–64.

Sanneh, Lamin. "The Domestication of Islam and Christianity in African Societies: A Methodological Approach." *Journal of Religion in Africa*, 1980: pp. 1–12.

Searing, James. "Conversion to Islam: Military Reruitment and Generaltional Conflict in a Sereer-Safen Village (Bandia), 1920–38." *Journal of African History* 44, no. 1 (2003): pp. 73–94.

Shank, David. "The Taming of the Prophet Harris." *Journal of Religion in Africa*, 1997: pp. 59–95.

Streusand, Douglas. "What Does Jihad Mean?" *Middle Eastern Quarterly*, September 1997.

Umar, Muhammad. "Muslims' Eschatological Discourses on Colonialism in Northern Nigeria." *Journal of the American Academy of Religion* 67, no. 1 (1999): pp. 59–84.

Wilkinson, David. "Spatio-Temporal Boundaries of African Civilizations Reconsidered." *Annual Meeting of the International Society for the Comparative Study of Civilizations*. Scranton, Pennsylvania, 1993. pp. 59–90.

Willis, John R. "Jihad fi Sabil Allah- Its Doctrinal Basis in Islam and Some Aspects of its evolution in Nineteenth Century West Africa." *Journal of African History*, 1967: pp. 395–415.

Zempleni, A. "La dimension therapeutique du culte des rab Ndep Tuuru et Samp: Rites de possession chez les lebou et les wolofs." *Psychopathologie Africaine*, 1966: pp. 395–439.

Zempleni, Andras. "L'enfant nit ku bon: Un tableau psycho-pathologique traditionnel chez les Wolof et Lebou du Sénégal." *Psychopathologie Africaine* 1, no. 3 (1965): pp. 329–441.

Books

Abun-Nasr, Jamil M. *Muslim Communities of Grace: The Sufi Brother hoods in Islamic Religious Life*. New York: Columbia University Press, 2007.

Armstrong, Karen. *Islam: A short history*. New York: Random House, 2002.

Babou, Cheikh Anta. *Fighting the Greater Jihad: Ahmadu Bamba and the founding of the Muridiyya of Senegal, 1853–1913*. Athens, Ohio: The Ohio University Press, 2007.

Balandier, G. and P. Mercier. *Les pecheurs Lebou du Senegal: particularisme et evolution*. Dakar: Centre d'IFAN, 1952.

Barry, Boubacar. *Le royaume de Waalo: le Senegal avant la conquete*. Paris: Karthala, 1985.

—. *Senegambia and the Atlantic Slave Trade*. Trans. Ayi Kwei Armah. Cambridge UK: Cambridge University Press, 1998.

Clarke, Peter. *Mahdism in West Africa:The Ijebu Mahdiyya Movement*. London: Luzac Oriental, 1996.

—. *West Africa and Islam: A study of religious development from the 8th to the 20th century*. London: Edward Arnold Ltd., 1982.

Cleveland, William L. *A History of the Modern Middle East.* Boulder: Westview Press, 1994.

Cohen, William. *The French Encounter with Africans: White Responses to Blacks, 1530–1880* (Bloomington, Indiana: University of Indiana Press, 2003

Davidson, Basil. *Africa in History.* New York: Touchstone, 1995.

Diop, Cheikh Anta. *Pre-Colonial Black Africa.* Translated by Harold Salemson. Brooklyn, NY: Lawrence Hill Books, 1987.

Diouf, Mamadou. *Le Kajoor au XIX eme Siecle: pouvoir ceddo et conquete coloniale.* Paris: Karthala, 1990.

Dumez, Richard and Moustapha Ka. *Yoff le territoire assi é g é : Un village l é bou dans la banlieue de Dakar.* Paris: L'Organisation des Nations Unies pour l'education, la science, et la technology, 2000.

Eze, Emmanuel, ed. *Race and the Enlightenment: A Reader.* Oxford: Blackwell Publishers, 2001.

Genova, James. *Colonial Ambivalence, Cultural Authenticity, and theLimitations of Mimicry in French-Ruled West Africa, 1914–1956.* New York: Peter Lang Publishing, Inc, 2004.

Gomez, Michael. *Pragmatism in the Age of Jihad: The Pre-Colonial State of Bundu.* Cambridge: Cambridge University Press, 1992.

Gordon Darnell Newby, *The Making of the Last Prophet: A reconstruction of the earliest biography of Muhammad.* Columbia, SC: University of South Carolina Press, 1989.

Hall, Gwendolyn Midlo. *Africans in Colonial Louisiana: the Development of Afro-Creole Culture in the Eighteenth Century.* Baton Rouge: Louisiana State University Press, 1995.

Harrison, Christopher *France and Islam in West Africa, 1860–1960.* Cambridge: Cambridge University Press, 1988.

Hiskett, Mervyn. *The Course of Islam in African History.* Edinburgh: University of Edinburgh Press, 1994.

Laborde, Cecile. *La Confriereie Layenne et les Lebou du Senegal: Islam et culture traditionnelle en Afrique.* Bordeaux: CEAN, 1995.

Lings, Martin, *Muhammad: His life based on the earliest sources.* Cambridge, UK: Islamic Texts Society, 1995

Mbacke, Khadim. *Sufism and Religious Brotherhoods in Senegal.* Translated by Eric Ross. Princeton, NJ: Markus Weiner Publisher, 2005.

O'Brien, Donal B. Cruise. *The Mourides of Senegal: the political and economic organization of an Islamic brotherhood.* Oxford: Clarendon Press, 1971.

Robinson, David. *Muslim Societies in African History.* Cambridge: Cambridge University Press, 2004.

—. *Paths to Accommodation: Muslim Societies and French Colonial Authorities in Senegal and Mauritania, 1880-1920.* Athens, Ohio: Ohio State University Press, 2000.

—. *The Holy War of Umar Tal: The Western Sudan in the mid-nineteenth century.* New York: Oxford University Press, 1985.

Said, Edward *Orientalism* New York: Pantheon, 1978.

Samb, Amar. *Essai sur la contribution du Senegal à la literature d'expression arabe.* Dakar: IFAN, 1972.

Sanneh, Lamin. *Disciples of all Nations: Pillars of World Christianity.* New York: Oxford University Press, 2008.

—. *The Jakhanke: the history of an Islamic clerical peoples of the Senegambia.* London: International African Institute, 1979.

Sarr, El Hajj Malik. *Ajibou da Iyallah ou La vie exemplaire de Limamou Laye.* Dakar: Imprimerie Nouvelle, 1966.

Sobel, Mechal. *Trablin' On: The Slave Jouney to an Afro-Baptist Faith.* Princeton: Princeton University Press, 1979.

Sylla, Assane. *La face cachée de l'exil de Seydina Limamou Lahi al Mahdi à Gorée.* Dakar: Fondation Seydina Issa Rouhou Lahi, Mouvement des Jeunes, 1991.

—. *Le peuple lebou de la presqu'île du Cap-Vert.* Dakar: Les Nouvelles Editions Africaines du Senegal, 1992.

—. *Les Prophetes Seydina Limamou Le Mahdi et Seydina Issa Rouhou Lahi.* Dakar: Imprimerie Saint-Paul, 1989.

Trimingham, J. Spencer. *Islam in West Africa.* Oxford: Clarendon, 1959.

Weber, Max. *Max Weber On Charisma and Institution Building.* Chicago: Uninversity of Chicago Press, 1968.

Index